729

D0070328

DRESS   REHEARSAL

OTHER BOOKS BY QUENTIN REYNOLDS

The Wounded Don't Cry

London Diary

Convoy

Only the Stars Are Neutral

View of Dieppe

QUENTIN REYNOLDS

DRESS REHEARSAL

33540

The Story of Dieppe

RANDOM HOUSE : NEW YORK

FIRST PRINTING

To GINNY and JOANIE (of course)

FOREWORD

HAD I any sense of objectivity (which I have not) and were asked to review this book (an unlikely contingency) I would pick out several flaws in it. I would say:

"The author has put entirely too much of himself in this book and not enough of Dieppe. It purports to be the story of the raid on Dieppe, yet the pages are filled with trivia not connected directly with the raid at all. Now and then the facetiousness with which the author treats certain aspects of the Dieppe operation jars one's

sensibilities. He begins, for instance, with the story of six pork chops. He then gives us a rather overlong account of how he as a reporter managed to go along with the raiders. He wastes a couple of thousand words telling us about Vice Admiral, the Lord Louis Mountbatten. During the raid he apparently spent more time talking to the wounded than getting the factual data which might give us a clearer idea of what went on during those nine hours at Dieppe. The book presents little in the way of new or "inside" information about the Dieppe raid. For the most part it presents the author's reactions to the events. His obvious admiration for his fellow correspondents is reflected in the several anecdotes about their behavior under fire, but none of this is of any value to the serious student of military affairs. It is, in short, the kind of narrative that one of the Rover Boys might have written, had he accompanied the raiders. For the real, comprehensive story of Dieppe, as a military operation, we shall have to wait for the historians."

I plead guilty on all counts, and present this brief preface so that the reader looking for a profound dissertation on Dieppe will not waste his time with the following pages. To me Dieppe began with the problem of how to wangle my way on the raid, and the six pork chops mentioned played their part in this phase of it. I have treated certain aspects of the raid facetiously because that is how the actual fighting men involved

treated them. I have given a picture of Mountbatten because I think he is a remarkable man,
and because children a hundred years from now
will be studying his life and discussing his achieve-
ments as they now study campaigns of Stonewall
Jackson. Mountbatten, always called the C. C. O.
(Commander Combined Operations), has that
indefinable something called color, the thing that
made Babe Ruth a household name and Lou
Gehrig just another great baseball player; sports
writers for years have been trying to describe
color and none have succeeded. Jack Dempsey had
it and Enrico Caruso had it. Obscure Floyd Col-
lins dying in a cave in Tennessee had it, and
somehow or other Sergeant York never did have
it. General MacArthur has it and General Marshall hasn't. Ernest Hemingway drips with color
while John Steinbeck is just a great writer. Clark
Gable would be the first to raise his hands in
horror if called a great actor but he's got color—
Paul Muni hasn't. You can't rationalize or explain it. But you can recognize it. And Mountbatten has got it to the nth degree. That's why
he'll be remembered.

Once we arrived at Dieppe it was difficult to
be objective, certainly the first requisite of any

historian. Very soon the operation became a fight for survival on the part of every man engaged— German as well as Canadian—British—or American. When this happens, the objective reporter forgets his objectivity very quickly. The whole affair becomes strictly personal, and I know of no other way to write about it. Fear, pain, horror, pity—these all swirled around us at Dieppe and each in turn took hold of every one of us and gripped us, leaving no room for objective thinking. When the war has been over for a few years, those of us who have been in fairly direct contact with it, will, I am sure, sit down and be objective as hell. We will write long, and I know dull, treatises on the profound issues which were at stake. That will be easy to do then. It isn't so easy for us to do that now.

My colleagues in London, in Moscow and in Cairo feel as I do. I know because we have often talked over this common failing we all have— this inability to be the objective reporters we all were not so long ago. To us the war presents no complex problem at all. After three years of it, we hate Germans and are very happy when we see Germans killed. We know that our cause cannot prevail until many thousands of Germans are killed—and I mean German "civilians" (if there are any such)—as well as German armed men. Viewing the war with that state of mind, it is not difficult to see how we lost our objectivity. Long ago the objectivity was bombed and shelled out of us. The story of Dieppe, like the story of every operation I have been on, is therefore a personal story and not intended to be a historical document for use in the War College.

There is even some fiction in the following pages. Not much—but some. This book was submitted to Mountbatten's office for censorship. I could not use the real name of the radio genius who was to be shot by his own troops, rather than be captured. So I invented the name *Wendell* for him. That, as far as memory serves, is the only fiction in the book, but under the mental stress of nine hours such as we spent in the harbor it is quite likely that in some cases I have exaggerated or unduly dramatized incidents not important in themselves. Anyhow, there you are.

1

WHY no poet has ever sung an ode to the pork chop I do not know. It is true that Charles Lamb wrote a little dissertation on roast pig once, but the poets have shied away from such delightful subjects as chops. There was a time when I could take my pork chops or leave them alone. In fact, I am sure that I spent many consecutive months without ever thinking of pork chops. But that was before London— 1942. Food in London these days is as monoton-

3

ous as a Sunday morning radio program. It is true that nobody starves in London; in fact, everyone gains weight. You gain weight because the food you are given is fattening if uninteresting. You can always get game in season and there are always plenty of potatoes, brussels sprouts and cabbage. I have seen sprouts and cabbage in their native state decorating the hats of the John Powers models, and very cute they look too. As a means of expressing disapproval of a bad burlesque play, I know of nothing better than sprouts or cabbage. But as an integral part of one's diet they leave much to be desired. Usually we end up in London eating meat and potatoes, a diet frowned upon by the purists in matters of nutrition. The choice of meat is strictly limited to mutton, liver, sweetbreads, game and an occasional tired chicken. After many many months of this succulent diet, a pork chop looks like something that dropped from heaven.

I live at the Savoy Hotel here in London and the food at the Savoy is no better than it should be. Now and then the Savoy surprises you. One morning, for instance, my floor waiter burst into my room very early to awaken me with a gleeful cry that he could get me scrambled eggs for

4

breakfast. Such an occasion would be excuse enough to awaken Winston Churchill at four in the morning. I hadn't seen an egg for months. The waiter hurried off and soon returned with a beautiful-looking dish of scrambled eggs. He stood beside the table he had brought in, gazing lovingly at them. It was, in fact, quite an occasion. But I tasted the scrambled eggs. I spit out the scrambled eggs. I cursed the scrambled eggs.

"This is scrambled sawdust," I told the waiter reproachfully. "A chicken would die of shame if you said she was responsible for this mess."

"Oh, no," he said, almost crying. "It's scrambled eggs. They're made out of that new egg powder they sent from America."

"You woke me up for that!" I yelled at him. "Taste them! Send them back to America!"

But sometimes the Savoy does do better than that. There was the morning when Santarelli, the Savoy maître d'hôtel, phoned in high excitement to tell me that he had located six pork chops and that he was saving them for me. I will never forget those six pork chops. It was through them that I met Vice Admiral, the Lord Louis Mountbatten. It was through them that I managed to get on the Dieppe raid when all other means of taking part in a Commando operation had failed. It happened like this:

When the Commando raids began I was at home for a brief vacation. The British War Office, which handles press facilities for all operational trips involving the British Army, called in the American press. The War Office would allow two, or in some cases, three members of the press to accompany the Commandos on their operations. As to which correspondents should go was a matter to be decided by the Press itself. Ray Daniell, president of the Association of American Correspondents in London, met with the executive committee of our Association, and decided upon a rota system. Lots should be drawn. Those at the head of the list should go first. The others would take their turns. It was a fair and sensible arrangement. But I was in New York at the time and never had a chance to draw. When I returned to London I was very much out in the cold. The War Office was regretful, but, after all, the American correspondents had made the rule. Ray Daniell was sympathetic, but what could he do? Lots had already been drawn and the list made up.

A curious relationship exists among the correspondents in London. We are all great friends, and when our Association makes a rule we obey it. Although I was a member of the Association, I was not in direct competition with any of the boys. They all (except the *Time* and *Life* members) worked for daily newspapers or news services, while I wrote only for *Collier's Weekly*. I mentioned that to Ray.

"Suppose I can wangle my way on one of these raids?" I asked. "Would the boys resent it?"

"If it meant that one of them was kicked off to make room for you, of course they'd resent it," Daniell said.

That was reasonable enough too. For three years we'd all been working together and never had there been any friction. Men like Ed Beattie of the U.P., Bill Stoneman of the *Chicago Daily News*, Drew Middleton formerly of the AP, now of the *New York Times*, and the rest—had always played fair and had often helped me get facilities which I, as a correspondent for a weekly magazine, did not strictly rate.

"Suppose," I asked Ray, "that I go on some raid as an added starter?"

"Well, that's up to Mountbatten," he said

doubtfully. "If you can manage it so that no one is tossed off, I don't think anyone will mind."

Obviously the first thing to do was to meet Mountbatten. Two good friends of mine were working for Mountbatten at his Combined Operations Headquarters in Whitehall. They were Major Jock Lawrence and Lieutenant Douglas Fairbanks, Jr. Lawrence had been in Hollywood just a few months before, working for Sam Goldwyn. He was now a sort of press relation officer acting as liaison between Combined Operations and the American army and American press. The elder Fairbanks had always been a great friend of Mountbatten's and, when the Navy Department picked young Douglas to be temporarily attached to the Combined Operations Staff, Mountbatten was delighted. For several months Douglas had been on convoy (and nasty convoy) duty, which included duty in the Mediterranean as well as duty on Russia-bound convoys.

When Santarelli phoned with his news of six pork chops, I immediately thought of Jock and Douglas. Perhaps either or both could arrange for me to see Mountbatten. Before the war he was "Dickie" Mountbatten and I might have met him with any one of fifty friends of mine in New York

8

or Long Island—but never had. But now he was Vice Admiral, the Lord Louis Mountbatten, Commander in Chief of Combined Operations—and reporters did not barge into his office any time they happened to be in the vicinity of Whitehall. But Jock and Douglas might arrange it.

I phoned them and asked them to dinner. Both had engagements that evening. When I told them I had the only six pork chops in Britain waiting for them, they broke their engagements. I told Santarelli to really put it on good for us. He did. Neither Jock nor Douglas is much of a drinking man, but I did get enough Noilly Pratt Vermouth (virtually non-existent in London) to make at least three good martinis—and I did get a bottle of champagne.

Anyone who would eat not one, but two, chops at a meal would certainly be guilty of evading the food rationing laws. He would, in fact, be in every sense of the word a slacker and worthy of nothing but contempt. I decided to be a slacker and worthy of nothing but contempt. I told Santarelli that there would be six of us. He said he'd have the chops breaded and that they'd be ready at eight thirty promptly. Jock and Douglas arrived on time. We had our cocktails in my

9

apartment, and for a time it was pleasant to talk about pals of ours in Hollywood and New York. I didn't quite know what Douglas did at Combined Operations, but you soon learn not to ask questions of that nature even of your best friends. We talked of Irving Asher, Hollywood producer, who had just arrived in London. I asked if Irving was well-heeled. Douglas assured me that he was. I made a mental note of that. Some of my Eagle Squadron boys were a bit behind in their mess bills, and I was looking for angels to take care of them. I might add that later when I told Asher what I wanted, he merely asked, "How much do the kids need?" We talked of Willie Wyler, who was now Major William Wyler, and of his picture, *Mrs. Miniver,* which was such a hit in London. We talked of Commander John Ford, one of the greatest of all directors, who was in London making pictures for the navy, and of my great friend, Lieutenant John McClain, who was en route. We talked of Major David Niven, who was the first British subject in America to rush to join the British army when war broke out, of Hollywood writer Major Cy Bartlett, now aide to General Spaatz in London and of Colonel Darryl Zanuck who is with the Signal

10

Corps. All in all we decided that Hollywood had done a pretty good job.

"It's getting so when you walk into Claridges you think you're in the Brown Derby," Lawrence said.

"I think the food is a little better at the Brown Derby than anywhere in London," Fairbanks said thoughtfully. "Unless you're on the level about those breaded pork chops."

"Let's get moving," I suggested.

We walked into the dining room of the Savoy. Santarelli greeted us with a beaming smile. He had served Douglas' father a hundred times, and it was a pleasure for him to serve Lieutenant Douglas, Jr. His face fell when he saw there were only three of us.

"It's a pity," I said dolefully. "But I had three other officers coming and they were unexpectedly called back to duty."

"But I have six big chops all ready," Santarelli moaned.

"Oh, well," I patted him on the shoulder. "We'll make the best of it. Just serve us two chops each instead of one. We won't mind."

"Very clever," Douglas said admiringly.

11

"there's more ham in you than in any actor I know."

Santarelli hurriedly removed three of the chairs and we three sat down and ate our pork chops and mashed potatoes (smothered with margarine), our beets and our beans, and felt very happy indeed. They were thick, lovely pork chops, cooked beautifully, and when I saw the satisfied expressions on the faces of Douglas and Jock I knew that this was the time to strike.

"You know I'd love to meet your boss," I said casually. "It's funny, but I've never met Mountbatten."

"He's a great guy," Lawrence said. "Maybe we could arrange it."

"It would have to be completely off the record," Douglas said. "The C.C.O. hates publicity. Stories about his work and about Combined Operations only embarrass him."

"I just want to meet him, that's all," I said innocently.

Fairbanks looked at me suspiciously. "You're not working on some angle, are you?"

"Really, Douglas," I said, very hurt. "You know me better than that. Hell, I can't even go on a Commando raid because I wasn't here when the boys drew lots. I'd love to go on one of those operations but I know the rules."

"We both know you better than that," Lawrence said. "All right, so you've given us a swell meal. You want to meet the C.C.O. Sure. I don't blame you. The question is, does he want to meet you?"

"We could forward a merely routine request to him, saying you would like a few minutes with him," Douglas said. "On the understanding that everything is off the record. That's as far as we can go."

"Well, do your best," I said and let it go at that.

Two days later my phone rang and a voice said, "This is the Flag Lieutenant of the C.C.O. If you could be at Headquarters at four this afternoon the C.C.O. would be glad to see you."

I said I'd be there and I was. I stopped to see Lawrence in his office to thank him for arranging it. "I had nothing to do with it," he mumbled. "I imagine Douglas fixed it."

I went in to see Douglas and thanked him. "It wasn't me," Douglas said cheerfully. "But for God's sake remember when you see him anything he says is off the record."

Neither of my pals wanted the responsibility

13

of arranging for me to see the Boss. Actually their hesitancy was typical of the discipline, the esprit de corps and the mental attitude of Mountbatten's staff. Each man was trained to mind his own business and not to encroach on some one else's domain. Each man was absolutely schooled to secrecy. Neither Lawrence nor Fairbanks, nor any of the other staff members, ever said anything to me about the activities of Combined Operations that the German Gestapo couldn't have listened to without learning a thing. Mountbatten had the quality of making his men into images of himself. Security—security—security—that was drummed into them until they must have heard the word in their dreams. The result justifies their caution—to date no word ever got around of any advance Commando operation.

Mountbatten lives up to advance notices. He doesn't let you down when you meet him. So many heroes do. Mountbatten is tall, with pale-blue eyes and a wide mouth that smiles readily, but which can tighten into a thin, uncompromising, straight line. Let's consider the career of this amazing man for a moment. He figures more prominently each day. He will figure very prominently in any future offensive operations taken

14

by the United Nations in the European theatre
of war. In his lifetime he has become a legend in
the Royal Navy and among the people of Britain.
And yet he started life with two strikes on him; he
had practically all the cards stacked against him.
He had too many rich relatives of royal blood.

Assiduous readers of the society pages were
quite familiar with the name of Mountbatten long
before the war. Little of what they read would
have led them to believe that he might emerge
as Public Hero No. 1 in any war. Mountbatten's
pedigree practically drips with royal ermine. His
older brother was the Marquess of Milford Haven.
His father was German-born Prince Louis of
Battenberg and his mother, Princess Victoria, was
the daughter of Louis IV, Grand Duke of Hesse,
and of Princess Alice, the daughter of Queen
Victoria. That all made a beautiful tune for the
pre-war Newport or Long Island hostesses to play
on their tiaras. In addition, Mountbatten is the
second cousin of King George VI.

During the 1860's Mountbatten's father became
a naturalized British subject. He translated
"Battenberg" to its English equivalent of "Mountbatten." In the early days of the last war he was
made First Sea Lord, but the war hysteria of 1914

made the public forget that for forty-six years he had been a loyal British subject, and he resigned from his job. He died in 1921, leaving a young son in the Royal Navy to carry on the tradition without the handicap of a Teutonic name. The young son, then just "Dickie" Mountbatten, had begun his career at the ripe old age of thirteen and he slung his hammock as a midshipman on *H. M. S. Lion*. But Lord Louis, after the last war, divided his time between night clubs and Cannes, and pacing the quarterdeck of a naval ship. The public might be pardoned for thinking of him as just another good-looking young glamour boy who belonged to the happy-go-lucky set led by his pal the Prince of Wales. Some of the newspaper clippings of the early thirties give a hint as to how Lord Louis spent much of his time.

> *(Herald Tribune,* 1933)
> Cannes, April 15. (A.P.) A feature of the Battle of Flowers here today was the loss of dignity, hat and stick by Lt. Com. Lord Louis Mountbatten. He had mislaid his ticket and, when police tried to eject him from the Royal Box, he resisted. A scuffle ensued which ended when the horrified Mayor of Cannes recognized and rescued the royal visitor.

The Story of Dieppe

(New York Times, 1931)

Lord Louis Mountbatten was severely shaken up by a fall from his pony during a polo game at Roehampton today. As he lay on the field, unconscious, his friend and house guest, King Alfonso, rushed from the stands to help carry his stricken host to a dressing room. Afterwards King Alfonso drove him to the Mountbatten home, Brook House, Park Lane, London, where he was said to be resting quietly.

When Lord and Lady Louis Mountbatten made periodic visits to the United States, society chroniclers had more fun. Mountbatten, looking like a cross between the Duke of Kent and Leslie Howard, was popular on both sides of the Atlantic. So was the beautiful and gracious Lady Mountbatten, Edwina Ashley (named for her godfather King Edward VII), whom Mountbatten had married in 1922. These two had been well endowed by the gods. The war was to prove how really lavish the gods had been in their gifts. But in the careless days they graced the late spots in London; they popularized pink champagne at Antibes; they gambled casually at Monte Carlo and often went half way round the world to keep engagements with their very great friend, Douglas

Fairbanks, Sr.; Fred Astaire and other stage and film stars were their guests, and occasionally they varied the routine by dining with King George and Queen Mary. These were the Mountbattens the world knew before war was declared. Actually no more distorted picture of them could have been imagined. Now and then his pals on gay parties had their doubts of Lord Louis. Occasionally he acted queerly. There was that time, for instance, when he was missed for a long period and they discovered that he'd been at Cambridge getting a degree in electrical engineering. Then too he was always inventing "gadgets" usually having to do with ships or this new thing called "wireless" which the Americans called "radio." To be serious-minded was a crime in the twenties and early thirties. When the war came the Mountbattens shed their gaiety and their casual smiles. This was their destiny and both found themselves equal to the demands of it. Lady Louis Mountbatten immediately donned the uniform of a civilian defense worker.

And Mountbatten went to work. We first heard of Mountbatten as a brilliant naval leader in 1939. He was in command of the destroyer *H. M. S.*

18

Kelly when it was hit by a mine in the Channel. There wasn't much left of the ship, but by some miraculous seamanship Mountbatten got her home. She was repaired and lived to fight another day. He had her back in service within a few months, but her back luck continued. This time a torpedo found her narrow eggshell of a hull in the North Sea. It took Mountbatten ninety hours to bring her home, but he got her there. This ship died hard. Mountbatten didn't wait for them to repair *Kelly*. He went out on *H. M. S. Javelin*, another destroyer, but *Javelin* too stopped a torpedo in a Channel engagement. Again Mountbatten refused angrily to abandon ship. Somehow he got the battered hulk to port. They gave him the D. S. O. then, and no one even suggested that the fact he had royal relatives had anything to do with it. Instead, sailors in wardrooms said, "About time, too."

Kelly, looking new again in her war paint, was ready for trouble again, and Mountbatten went back to his real love. He fought her in the Mediterranean, and then off Crete a Nazi dive-bomber got her—but good. Steel and blast struck deep in her belly and the *Kelly* came apart at the seams. There was no question now of "abandoning ship."

The *Kelly* just folded up and then sank. Mount-batten and some survivors clung to a rubber raft, spitting oil and hoping that there were no sharks in the neighborhood. I remember how the pilots at Malta hated the thought of having to bail out in the Mediterranean. They worried more about sharks than they did about Messerschmitts or Focke-Wulfs. Many of them always carried a small pistol. This was "just in case." They'd rather put a bullet through their brains than risk being mauled by sharks. But Mountbatten survived the sharks and the chill and another destroyer soon picked him and his mates up.

"Funny thing," he said as they hauled him aboard and wiped the oil from his smarting eyes, "how sure you are that you'll survive yourself."

The Noel Coward film, *In Which They Serve* is more than the fictionized version of a naval captain. It is the story of Mountbatten, and "Captain D" in the picture reflects the spirit, the courage and the methods of Mountbatten. No better description of Mountbatten can be given than the one Coward presents in his magnificent picture.

Mountbatten's hatred for the Germans became intensified into a cold white flame after that. He loved *Kelly;* he loved the shipmates he had lost and he mourned for two valuable keepsakes which had gone down. These were a picture of the King and the Queen and a silver cigarette box given him by the Duke of Windsor. Both were inscribed the same: "To dear Dickie—With Love." The Mountbatten who paced the foredeck of *Kelly,* cold-eyed, thin-lipped, calculating, could still spare a thought for those who had figured in his other life—that gay, laughing casual existence when he was "Dickie" to everyone in London.

Lord Louis' next stop was the United States, but it wasn't for fun and games, and the unhappy Long Island, Washington and Newport hostesses never received answers to the hysterical invitations they sent him. They wouldn't have known this Mountbatten anyway. They didn't talk his language any more. He was a sailor now—nothing else. His new job was to take over the aircraft carrier, *Illustrious*, which was being repaired in a Norfolk shipyard. Oddly enough, the only battle scar Mountbatten ever received was at Norfolk, when he went to inspect the *Illustrious*. The good citizens of Norfolk gave the crew of the *Illustrious* a goat for a mascot. Mountbatten was introduced to the goat, who looked suspiciously at the gold braid. The goat curbed his impatience until Mountbatten turned his back—always a strategical error. Then the goat lowered his head and charged. Contrary to the general rule, this was not a butting goat—but a biting goat. He nipped Mountbatten's leg and trotted off triumphantly with a bit of Mountbatten's trouser leg in his mouth.

Lord Louis persuaded Walt Disney to design an emblem for his new ship. Disney drew a sketch of Donald Duck dressed as an admiral standing and holding a model airplane flying the Union Jack. But then Mountbatten disappeared. He bobbed up in London and we wondered what had happened. We heard that he was doing some hush-hush job. We never saw him in London. Neither did his colleagues at his clubs—Brook's or Marlborough. Actually he was going to school. His chief instructors were books on guerrilla warfare, naval landings, assault parties and the tactics employed by the Boer shock troops in South Africa. Then he went to live and train with the men whom he was to command in the future. He went through the Commando training which he himself had helped to institute. It is a vigorous back-breaking training and only a small percentage of those who begin the Commando course survive it.

A Commando trooper begins where an ordinary infantryman leaves off. He starts in perfect physical condition and with the usual knowledge and training of any good soldier. Then he learns amphibious warfare, how to swim with full equipment, how to land safely from all kinds of craft and how to handle these craft. He learns guerrilla warfare, signaling, the use of radio communication, fieldcraft, the proper use of explosives and how to apply them to barbed-wire entanglements and other barriers. The ordinary infantryman carries a pair of shears to cut barbed wire, but no shears can cut their way through the kind of barbed wire with which Germans protect their beaches. If you encounter a wall which is surmounted by barbed wire two feet high and three feet thick, only explosives will do the trick. Commandos carry Farington torpedos with them and they know just how much of this deadly weapon to use in any given emergency. They are trained in the use of German weapons so that any they capture may be turned against the enemy. They are walking arsenals once they swing into action —carrying grenades, revolvers, rifles, knives, tommy guns and ropes. They learn how to creep up quietly on an enemy and how to put him out of action without any noise being made. They are the best-trained group in the world—they are trained to murder, and beautiful murderers they are. Sometimes, such as on the Lofoten and Dieppe raids they wear heavy stout shoes. Then again as at Boulogne, they wear rubber-soled shoes. Each raid demands different weapons, different tactics. Sometimes they wear steel helmets; more often they wear black or brown stocking headgear. Usually they black their faces on raids. Every precaution against premature discovery is made.

We correspondents still wondered what Mountbatten was doing. We didn't know that Winston Churchill had placed him in charge of this new suicide group which Churchill himself, refreshing his Boer war memories, had named the Commandos, just as the Boers had named them nearly forty years before.

Incidentally a Commando is not an individual soldier, but a military unit approximating a battalion. However, public usage has upset the military dictionary and any man who is a member of Mountbatten's command is called a Commando, and there is nothing that Mountbatten can do about it. He himself never uses the term. He calls his command Combined Operations, a part of which are some Commando detachments.

Finally the news leaked out that Mountbatten was the boss of this amazing group which had so captured the imagination of the public and of Fleet Street.

From the beginning, the deeds of the Commandos were shrouded in secrecy. We correspondents for months were not allowed to watch their training tactics. When they raided, they made quick sharp jabs at enemy positions and invariably the raid was over before any of us knew about it. The first raid took place on March 4, 1941, and the target was the shipping center in the Lofoten Islands. Beyond the brief announcement that the raid "had very substantial results" little else was learned. Then came the Vaagso raid on Norway, and Mountbatten saw us this time and described the operation. He was a little disappointed about one thing.

"Our timing went a bit adrift," he said disconsolately. "We were due to land at 8:30. Actually the first man was not ashore until 8:31."

He preaches timing, timing, timing to his officers. There must be perfect synchronization between land, sea and air forces for a raid to succeed. We found that out at Dieppe and we realized then how even a one-or two-minute lag can upset a whole planned schedule. After Vaagso came the second Lofoten raid, and raids on Bruneval, St. Nazaire and Boulogne followed.

By now we realized that the Commando operations were eventually to be more than mere annoying pinpricks against the thick-skinned German defenses. We tried to find out more and more about the operations of Mountbatten and his men but we came up against a wall of polite silence. We got to know many of Mountbatten's staff but they never unbent. And the Mountbatten legend grew. It became known that he had accompanied his men on more than one raid. When a second front was discussed, his name always came up and we wondered if eventually he wouldn't be the man to command the whole British-American forces. He had three titles: Vice Admiral, Honorary Lieutenant General and Honorary Air Marshal.

I had met Lady Louis Mountbatten in her capacity as Superintendent in Chief of the St. John's Ambulance Brigade several times, but I had never met Lord Louis. Before going into his office I chatted with one of his aides, Lieutenant Colonel Robert Parks - Smith of the Royal Marines, a handsome man who even looked dignified under the weight of one of those handle-bar mustaches. Affable, smiling Bobby Parks* said, "I hope you can come along with us some time. These raids are a lot of fun—when you come back."

Mountbatten sat behind a big desk, but he fitted it well. He arose, smiling, and shook hands the way a sailor shakes hands. His handclasp was hard and firm. Mountbatten is tall, with dark hair and eloquent eyes which narrow in concentration and then open wide when he laughs. He told me that Lawrence and Fairbanks had asked him to see me and then he paid a casual but sincere tribute to them both. "They're good men," he said briefly, which is a little bit like Joe Louis saying of another fighter, "He can sure hit." Mount-batten does not scatter praise around for the pur-pose of making conversation. Behind him on the wall were huge military maps of the French and Norwegian coasts. He talked of the raids that had taken place.

*Bobby Parks was at Dieppe with us, but he didn't have any fun because he didn't come back.

27

"Some came off," he said. "Some didn't. We can't always be successful. We'll have more of them. That's no secret. In fact we have virtually told the Germans that we intend to raid again. This we find has had the effect of making them withdraw some of their men and aircraft from Russia. That's fine. Anything that releases pressure on the Russians is good."

"I wish I could go along some time," I said, and he laughed.

"Yes, I thought so." he said dryly. "Well, why not? I have no objection. But that's all up to the War Office and your own colleagues. You see, we have room for only a certain number of correspondents. Sometimes it is only two or three. Sometimes we can take a few more along. We have already made arrangements for the men to be taken along on the next operation. Now, if at the last moment we have room for one more, I'll let you go along—that is, if you can fix it with the American press. We want to be fair about it."

"I think I can fix it."

"Good," he nodded briskly. There is nothing placid about Mountbatten. He talks quickly in a rather high voice. He makes quick gestures with his hands which are slender, yet slender as steel

28

can be slender and yet strong. He talked about the
way things worked on a raid. He described some
of the other raids and suddenly I found myself
leaning forward, completely gripped by the fasci-
nation of these tales of life and death. He went
on, and now I began to get an inkling of the
complicated plans that had to be made.

He talked about his reluctance to risk the
capture of anyone who might have information
of value to the enemy. Months before we had
heard from R.A.F. pilots who had escaped from
German hands how expert the Huns were in
getting the truth from prisoners. They had to
some extent given up the physical torture they
had practiced against the Poles, the Czechs and
the Norwegians. This was prompted by no
humanitarian motives. The Germans had merely
discovered something far more efficacious than
torture. They had a drug which seemed to have
come right out of the Sunday supplements or a
popular boys' book about Dick Tracy or Man-
drake the Magician. They administered this
harmless drug to a prisoner and thereafter the
unhappy victim could not lie nor could he fail to
answer any questions put to him. It was a sort of
truth serum, something on the line of the publi-

cized "twilight sleep," its effect being that the subconscious mind completely overrules the conscious mind. No strength of will was proof against it. This was the story told by escaped prisoners, and British scientists had verified that such a drug existed. If you really knew anything, you couldn't afford to be captured.

I left Mountbatten completely captivated by the man. There wasn't a false note in him. He was hard, cold, shrewd—the perfect war leader. He would not worry too much about casualties if the objective to be gained was important. The Germans had made the rules. You had to fight them under their rules of ruthlessness or you were licked before you started. His men were not supposed to surrender. Their destiny was to kill or be killed. They knew it when they volunteered for the so-called "Special Service," a term used by the War Office, which hated the name Commando.

I left Combined Operations walking on air— my only regret being that his conversation (beyond the casual remarks I've quoted) would forever have to be buried under the tombstone of so many stories which wore the inscription: "Off the Record."

2

I HAD to fix it with the War Office and with my colleagues. This wasn't difficult. As long as I was an added starter who wasn't taking anyone's place, the War Office didn't mind. Now all I had to do was to wait until the next raid. Not all of the planned raids had come off. Bill Stoneman had waited around ten or twelve days at a British port. He was with the Commandos, who were all set for a rather big raid. The weather turned bad and the raid never took place. But, according to the rota rules, Bill had had his turn so he had to go to the bottom of the list. The same happened to Ned Russell of the United Press. I hoped it wouldn't happen to me. I hadn't done a really good story all summer. I needed a good one badly. I was anxious to get home for a couple of months, but it was hard to justify a request for a vacation on the basis of the trivial stories I'd been writing for *Collier's*. If I could get one really exciting operational story, I could, in good conscience, leave London for a while.

One day I phoned the Associated Press and asked for Drew Middleton. He was out of town. I asked where he was and was told that his office didn't know; he was away on some "hush-hush" assignment. His office only knew that he had been sent to some British port to wait instructions. They had no idea what the story was—probably Drew was taking a trip on a destroyer. I knew that Drew and Larry Meier of International News Service were next at bat on a raid, so this looked as though something were brewing. When I called the INS office and found that Larry was "out of town" I felt sure that it wouldn't be long now. I was right. On the evening of August 17th, Jock Lawrence phoned and suggested that we have

32

dinner. We sat around after dinner and I went out into the Strand with him to help find him a cab. After dark, taxis are very scarce in London. We finally found one. Jock stepped in and said casually, "I'll buy you breakfast in the morning. About ten?"

"There never was a breakfast worth getting up for that early," I told Jock. "Thanks, but I'll pass that up."

"No, you won't, "he said, stepping into the cab. "Be at my office at ten in civilian clothes. Bring your uniform in a bag. Sweet dreams." And the taxi pulled away. I went up to my room to pack and dream sweet dreams. I packed, all right, but I didn't dream any sweet dreams.

If you operate in the war zone long enough without getting hurt, you must logically begin to believe in your good luck. A correspondent has little except his luck to use as protective armament. We are not allowed to carry guns. If we do and are captured, we forfeit the privileges our status as accredited war correspondents might give us. I had only carried a gun once since I'd been in the war zone. That was in Libya. I was with the First Royal Sussex, a good fighting British line regiment. They had stormed and captured a place called Sidi Omar, nothing but a raised hunk of sand in the desert, but a place of some strategic importance at the moment. Unfortunately, our regiment, while victorious, had moved a bit faster than the rest of the line and we found ourselves in a rather isolated position for two days, entirely surrounded by German and Italian detachments. We were shelled and dive-bombed viciously, and Colonel Desmond Young, my "conducting officer," now a prisoner of war in Italy, thought that this might be a prelude to an attack by tanks and infantry.

"This bunch will never surrender," he said thoughtfully. "It might be as well if you had a gun. It might come to our fighting our way through the lines, and the bullets that come our way won't be able to read that "War Correspondent" on your shoulder.

"Where'll I get a gun?" I asked helplessly.

"Lots of trenches around here," he said laconically. "Plenty of dead Italians and Germans in them. Hasn't been time to bury them. Take your pick, chum."

I found a trench that was well occupied. I found a German who had a gun hanging from his belt. I took the gun, an American-made Colt. While I

34

was at it, I went through the German's pockets and found a pack of cigarettes. They were filthy, black, issue cigarettes, but I hadn't smoked in three days and they were better than nothing. Technically this is called looting, and is punishable by something like death. Actually we called it "reprovisioning." I hung the gun on my belt and tried to make believe it wasn't there. But I couldn't get over the feeling that it might go off any minute. When no one was looking, I "broke" the gun and emptied the cartridges into my pocket. I felt much braver then. As far as guns are concerned I am a conscientious objector. When I was eleven, I shot my kid brother Jim with an air rifle. The little lead pellet hit one half an inch above his right eye, and I had nightmares about that for twenty years. I've never fired a gun since that time; I've never held one in my hand without wincing. Anyhow, although a tank attack did materialize at Sidi Omar it was not followed by an infantry charge and I never had to use my bulletless gun.

That is the only time on any front I ever carried a gun. I'd always found my luck sufficient. But my luck didn't sing any song of security to me this night. I tossed and pitched and had nightmares

and woke up sweating two or three times. I hadn't
had nightmares for some time, not since the
bombing of London stopped. During those horrible nights, nightmares were common occur-
rences with me and with many of my colleagues.
The bombing, the noise of the guns bothered us
more when we were asleep than when we were
awake.

I wouldn't mind any bombing very much if I
were sitting around a table with Bill Stoneman,
Helen Kirkpatrick, Bob Low, Mary Welsh, Ed
Beattie, Drew Middleton or any of a dozen others
who were in London during the blitz. It's when
you're alone that you really mind bombing, and
when you're asleep it's bad because your subconscious mind which you can control when you
are awake, now takes over and raises hell with
you. It was like that this night before Dieppe.

When my secretary came in at nine thirty the
next morning she was amazed to find me up,
dressed and packed. My "hunch" still lay heavily
on me. I had none of that excited, exuberant feeling I'd had at Sidi Omar, or at Beauvais in France
when things were really hot, or when I flew with
the RAF night fighters or crossed the Atlantic in
convoy. I wondered if my luck had run out. I

felt as a man does who has made three straight passes with the dice. You hesitate to really shoot the works on that fourth pass. I tried to shake this absurd feeling of impending ill fortune off, but it persisted, and finally I had to succumb to it.

"This is the time I'm going to get it," I thought, with a curious feeling of detachment. Like all men with any imagination I am superstitious. I play hunches and of course always forget the hunches that don't pan out and remember the hunches that do. Now I had a bad hunch and couldn't do anything about it. It was the first time that I'd ever had this kind of a hunch.

"I'll be away for a few days," I told my secretary. "I'm going around to inspect some new American airdromes. General Eisenhower is taking me around."

Her face lit up. "General Eisenhower," she breathed. "How wonderful!"

Betty Marais, who had been running my life in London for two years, just as any good secretary runs the life of her boss, was a name worshipper. When days passed without anyone of importance phoning me she would sulk and feel rather cheated. Then, if John Winant or Averell Harriman or Air Marshal Sir Sholto Douglas happened to phone, the sun was in the sky again and all was well with the world.

The phone rang and it was an old friend, Major Wally Giblin, of our Service of Supply. Betty took over.

"Quent is very busy," she said importantly. "He is leaving on a tour of inspection with General Eisenhower, the Commander in Chief of the American forces. Yes, General Eisenhower wants to know what he thinks of the airdromes built for the American pilots."

Before Betty could go on and probably invent a tale of how I had been asked to advise General Eisenhower on matters connected with the American forces, I grabbed the phone.

"Where's that case of Scotch you said you could get me?" I asked Giblin. Whisky had become very scarce in London. You could always buy a drink, but it was almost impossible to buy a bottle. I always had RAF boys dropping into my place and they could get rid of plenty of Scotch. I'd been ordering the usual "large whisky and soda" for them at about $1.10 a drink. Even the most robust expense account was no proof against such prices. Clever Wally Giblin had found a wine merchant who had some Scotch left.

38

He promised to go right to work on it. We chatted and, as I talked to him, my hunch came right back to hit me in the face. Suppose—just suppose—I was to get it? Who would pay my bills and wind up my affairs in London? It would be very untidy to have a lot of loose ends around. Giblin, of course, would be the perfect man to take care of things. When we finished talking I went to the typewriter and wrote a note to him.

Giblin had been a broker in civil life. I'd known him for years. He'd know how to handle things— just in case. I wrote:

> Dear Wally:
>
> I'm off on one of those trips. I don't anticipate any trouble, but there's always that hundred to one chance of getting it. In case I do, take care of things. I have about two hundred pounds in the Chase National Bank, Bush House Branch. Pay my bills at the Savoy and tip everyone. Betty will tell you the ones. I have some royalties coming from Cassell, my publishers. Show them this letter. It wil be authority for you to collect the money. Then somehow get it to Ginny in New York.
>
> Mind you, I don't think for a moment you'll have to use this letter but it seems silly not to consider the possibility of accident. And for the love of God, Wally, get me a case of Scotch as

I'm going broke feeding these Eagle boys drinks at a dollar a copy. I'll see you in a couple of days. There's a hell of a play just opened, called *Flare Path*. How about you and me and Russ Forgan seeing it Friday night? I'll go for the tickets if we can have dinner at your flat. And let Colonel Russ make the cocktails. Your idea of a martini seems to be one bottle of vermouth and one spoonful of gin.

All the best,
Quent.

I felt rather silly writing that letter, sealing it and giving it to Betty to be delivered by hand. But I felt satisfied, too, as you do when you take out theft insurance on your automobile. You don't expect your car to be stolen, but you feel better if you're insured against the possibility. I told Betty that I'd probably be gone about three days and I probably wouldn't be able to get in touch with her.

"That's fine," she said happily. "Vince and Bill are coming on leave the next three days. I'll tell them they can stay here."

Vince and Bill were two young American pilots who were alienating Betty's hitherto staunch loyalty to the RAF. Our American pilots certainly took London by storm—especially feminine London. They behave as well on leave in London as

40

they do in their aircraft, and you couldn't help but feel proud of them. Whenever I left town, Betty always found two or three pilots to occupy my suite. All of the American correspondents did the same thing. Hotel rooms in London are expensive and a pilot's pay doesn't quite run to them.

"I'm going to take them to Bea Lillie's show," Betty went on, "and then to the Nut House. We can sign your name there."

"I suppose you signed my name for the theatre tickets too."

"Oh, no," Betty said sweetly. "I phoned Bea and said you wanted three tickets for yourself, so we got them free."

Betty's bright impudence was one of the features of London. If Ed Beattie gave a party at the Savoy he'd get Betty to invite the guests, seat them and order the meal. If Wally Giblin wanted to send something home to his wife, he'd commandeer Betty to shop for him. Sometimes Betty's efficiency was absolutely startling. When Bob Riskin, the Hollywood writer, came to London to do some work for the Film Division of the Ministry of Information (gratis) I wanted to have a cocktail party for him. It would be fun, I thought, to have a piano player. I told Betty what

I wanted, told her to "invite the mob" and forgot about it. She really did herself proud. She remembered that Riskin had written *Mr. Deeds Comes to Town.* When our guests arrived they were startled to see a sign in the lobby of the Savoy which read, *Mr. Deeds Comes to London.* But Betty confessed that she couldn't find a piano player in all of London.

"But I had a piano moved into the room," she said casually, "and I invited the First Lord of the Admiralty to the party."

"You can't use cabinet ministers like that," I told her angrily.

"You don't have to ask Mr. Alexander to play," she said, hurt. "The piano is there and when he sees it, he'll just naturally walk over to it and play all night. You know how he loves to play the piano."

And of course that is what happened. A. V. Alexander is one of the hardest-working men in Britain. Other cabinet ministers find their relaxation in gardening, or moving pictures, or occasional spells of golf. Not Alex. When Alex is absolutely exhausted after perhaps a three-day stretch in the control room of the Admiralty, he relaxes at a piano. Alex knows the words and

42

music of more American college songs than anyone I ever met.

That is merely an example of the terrifying
efficiency of La Betty. And in addition to her
duties as social director and Mother Superior to
the RAF and the American Air Force, this twenty-
two-year-old youngster is the fastest and best
typist I ever saw.

The mail came and Betty handed me letters
from home. I put them in my pocket to read
later, grabbed the morning papers and left.

I had acquired a huge Packard car by now,
with driver. A wealthy British friend had lent me
the car for the duration. Cabs being so scarce,
especially at night, the car came in very handy.
I had my driver take me to the headquarters of
Combined Operations. I always winced a bit
when I drove there in my magnificent Packard.
There was a small space reserved for Mountbatten's car. It was there now. His car, which
he drove himself, was a small Morris that would
have fitted in my trunk rack. That was rather
typical of Mountbatten. I told my driver hurriedly
to beat it, as I wouldn't need him any more that
day. Hell, I might not need him ever again, I
thought, going into Headquarters.

You would never know anything was afoot by the conduct of the guards in the building. The secrecy in regard to raids was so well kept that very few even in the building knew of them in advance. On the second floor things were as usual. Girls in the uniforms of the Waafs, Wrens or Ats, moved unhurriedly through the halls. These girls, the pick of Britain's three women's services, acted as "personal aides" to Mountbatten's senior officers. They typed out schedules for raids; they, and they alone, knew everything that was planned. The girls were divided into two classes— "Secret" and "Most Secret." The girls in the latter class, of course, shared a terrific responsibility. They are all handpicked for their discretion and their trustworthiness.

Jock Lawrence was waiting for me. He brought me in to meet Colonel Bobby Parks-Smith who was to "brief" me. Parks-Smith looked handsome in his blue Marine uniform. He suggested that we might step over to the mess and have the "first today."

"Jock, I know, has told you of the urgent need for secrecy," he said. "You will go to Jock's apartment and change into your uniform there. A car will pick you up at two o'clock. It will drive you

44

to a port. There you will board the destroyer *Calpe*. Lieutenant Boyle, a nice young chap, will be expecting you. When the destroyer leaves its dock, he will tell you the whole story of where you're going. You will be the only correspondent on this ship. You'll be in a position to hear things and see things that you'll have to forget afterwards. You will be on the headquarters ship that directs the whole show. Captain Hughes-Hallett, R.N., will lead the naval part of the action from your ship. He expects you. When you return, there will be a car waiting for you. It will bring you directly here to Headquarters. Do not return to London by train, and talk to no one about the result of the operation until you have heard the C.C.O.'s orders. The other correspondents will be brought directly here too and the C.C.O. will hold a press conference at which you will be told just what the bans are and just what can be released. Got the form?"

I nodded, and he said cheerfully, "That's all. Now for that first one."

Attached to Headquarters was a room where you could get sandwiches and drinks. Parks-Smith, Lawrence and I ordered gin and limes and walked out on the terrace. It was a lovely morning and sitting there talking of recent movies we'd seen, it was difficult to face the reality of the immediate future. Colonel Robert Neville, of the Royal Marines, one of Mountbatten's most important aides, joined us. He talked of his last visit to America and about plays he had seen then.

"We've got no one here who can touch Cole Porter for writing lyrics," he said, and for a while the lyrics of Cole Porter seemed the most important thing in the world. We had "one for the road" and then they shook hands casually, said, "All the best," and Jock and I walked out to get a cab. The casual unhurried air about Headquarters and about Mountbatten's staff was typical of the way he operated. The details of this raid had all been worked out weeks before (I learned afterwards). There were no hasty last-minute improvisations. The work had all been done. From now on it was up to the operational force to adhere to the timetable and to carry out their assignments.

Lawrence and I bumped into Fairbanks as we left. Fairbanks looked at my bag and asked in surprise, "You off somewhere?"

"I'm making a tour with General Eisenhower,"

I told him, with a straight face. "May be gone a few days. I'll look you up when I get back."

"Fine," Fairbanks said, and then he shook hands and added, not so casually, "Lots of luck."

"Douglas knows damn well I'm not off on a trip with General Eisenhower," I said to Lawrence, when we got into the cab.

"Maybe he does. But Douglas has the gift of reticence or he wouldn't be working for the C.C.O."

We passed Charing Cross railroad station. In an effort to cut down unnecessary travel on the part of the civilian population, the government displays huge placards around all railroad stations. Jock pointed wordlessly at the poster showing a factory worker pointing his finger right at you, while the placard in large black type shouted, "Is Your Journey Necessary?"

"Probably by tonight I'll wish I'd stood in bed," I told Jock.

"You can take the boy out of Brooklyn, but you can't take the Brooklyn out of the boy," Lawrence said.

Lawrence and Colonel Loren B. Hillsinger, an American officer, had rooms in a lovely two-story house in Mayfair Mews. A mews is a sort of dead-end street. Originally these mews were lined with stables and ramshackle houses but some clever entrepreneur conceived the idea of making the mews respectable. Stables were done over and ancient houses strengthened, modernized and painted. The mews of London became fashionable. Lawrence lived in a beautiful house in one of them. He introduced me to tall, handsome Colonel Hillsinger, who was packing in a great hurry. He left and Jock laughed. "He's going on the same show you are going on. There will be several American observers along, and a few American troops—just a token force. And that's all I can tell you about the show."

I changed into my uniform. I was in battle dress I'd worn in Libya when I was accredited to the British Army there. It was very comfortable, if a bit unorthodox for this part of the world. I wore this instead of the heavier uniform we wore when with the British or American troops in Britain or in Ireland because of its light weight. In case this developed into a swimming race I didn't want to be handicapped by heavy clothes.

"Take off those war correspondent tabs," Jock said casually.

"What the hell for?" I was merely curious.

"You are going to a port and if all goes well,

48

the show will start tonight. Maybe weather will delay the show for a couple of days. If so, you'll stay at this port. If people saw you walking around with those two war correspondent tabs on your shoulders, they might figure there was some big show on. We don't want to take that risk. We'll replace them with a pair of lieutenant colonel's silver leaves. You'll be merely another American officer then."

"Why can't I be a general?"

"You're just not the type. No it would be very bad casting," Lawrence said, unpinning the regulation tabs from my shoulders and substituting the silver insignia of an American lieutenant colonel.

"I hope I meet some of these young American officers," I told Jock. "I'll have them saluting until their arms fall off."

I had a knapsack in my bag. I put in my toilet kit an extra shirt, a flashlight, a pair of socks, a pair of sun glasses, and two detective stories.

"That's all you'll need," Jock said. "With any luck, you'll be back within twenty-four hours. And if you don't have any luck, no extra clothes are going to help. Stay here until the car comes for you. There will be two officers going down

49

with you. I wouldn't ask them any questions about the operation."

I'd known Jock Lawrence in Hollywood when he did public relations and helped produce pictures for Sam Goldwyn. That was only a year before. That rather carefree, laughing Jock Lawrence had died—and in its place was this efficient, brisk, reticent American Major, who was all business. Jock lost some of his official demeanor when he said good-bye.

"I hope to Christ nothing happens to you," he said gravely. "But you're a pretty lucky guy."

"Sure, I'm a lucky guy," I said a bit doubtfully, not feeling very lucky at all. "You wouldn't have a bottle of Scotch around I could take along in case we run across any rattlesnakes in the Channel?"

"And how do you know you're going to be in the Channel?" he asked.

"I don't," I said, quite truthfully. "But stop confusing the issue. Have you a bottle of Scotch, or even of brandy? Answer yes or no."

He answered "No," very firmly and left, but not before he gave me two packs of Chesterfields and two packs of Camels as consolation prizes.

50

The Story of Dieppe

A few minutes later a car painted in dull brown squealed to a stop outside. I went out and climbed in the back. There were two officers there—one a Wing Commander and the other a British Major. We introduced ourselves and then the Wing Commander said to the driver, "Straight for Portsmouth."

"So that's where we take off from?" I suggested.

The Wing Commander looked at me, amazed. "Haven't you been briefed yet?"

"Not actually," I said. "I don't know where we're going or any of the details. I'm to be briefed when we get to the *Calpe.*"

This rather limited our conversation on the long ride to Portsmouth. It was a long ride—seventy-eight miles. But it was a beautiful day with the sun bathing the green fields of Devon and with August wearing a thousand varicolored flowers in her hair.

"Bad time to travel," the Wing Commander muttered.

"How's that?" I asked.

"At this time of day there's not a pub open the whole way from London to Portsmouth," he said darkly. "Very annoying, these license hours."

51

"We don't have any such nonsense in my country," I said proudly.

"You had prohibition, though," he said dryly.

"That's right, we did. Silly of us," I said, dismissing the subject hastily.

3

THE Portsmouth Navy Yard is an exciting place. It is one of the best-defended spots in Britain. I was caught there once during a blitz. The barrage the guns sent up against the Hun bombers was something to see and hear. In addition to the ordinary land ack-ack guns, every ship in the yard and the harbor began to blast. The Nazis haven't had much luck with Portsmouth, although they claim to have destroyed it twice.

Navy yards all over the world have something

in common. Portsmouth always reminds me of the Brooklyn Navy Yard. Drydocks all over the world look the same. But there, flanked by huge cranes, by the terrific din of riveting and with trucks rumbling over the cobblestones in front of it there is one beautifully anachronistic note. Immaculate in white, black and gold is the ancient *H.M.S. Victory* looking ready to sail again; looking contemptuously at the drab cruisers, destroyers and battlewagons around her. Nelson met his death at Trafalgar in 1805 in this old ship, and she stands there in drydock, an inspiration to the thousands of midshipmen who go through part of their training at Portsmouth.

Our driver knew where we were going. He stopped at one of the big stone or concrete pier heads. A warrant officer was waiting for us. He politely asked us for identification cards and gravely looked at them. Then he told us to wait for a few minutes. We sat on the end of the dock, talking about everything but the raid. It was a beautiful tribute to Mountbatten's code of secrecy that not once on the eighty-mile drive had either of my fellow-travelers said a word about the plans. I hadn't been "briefed"; therefore for the moment I was untouchable.

54

"There's a good hotel here," the Wing Commander said thoughtfully. "I had a steak there about a month ago. With onions."

I nodded. "The Queens? I slept there once for twenty hours."

"How was that?"

"I'd been on a Channel convoy during September, 1940. We went from Southend here to Pompey." Naval people never call Portsmouth anything but "Pompey."

"A lousy trip in those days," the Wing Commander said.

"It was a lousy trip. We got dive-bombed and slapped by E boats and then off Dover we got shelled. We landed here and I slept for twenty hours. I was on an armed trawler."

"How about that cocoa?"

I remembered the cocoa. "You could stick a spoon in it," I said nostalgically. "I never knew cocoa could be so good. It was there, standing on the stove all night and when you got cold you'd go in and dip a cup full out of the big pot. It's the best drink I know to take the chill out of you."

"That's why all navy ships issue it," the Wing Commander said. "But I'll take tea with rum in it. I used to carry brandy when I was flying, but

55

I switched to a thermos bottle filled with half-tea half-rum."

"You're a bomber pilot?"

He nodded. "Yes, fighter pilots don't have much chance to take a drink when they're in combat. Then at most they're only up for an hour and a half."

"The Russian pilots always carry vodka with them. I've known them to drink a whole bottle when they were up. It's pretty cold at 18,000 feet in Russia. The vodka warms them up."

"Vodka is a fraud," the Army Major broke in. "I was a year in Moscow and I got to know vodka very well. Nothing tough about it. It just tastes tough. Take grappa—there's a drink. Or slivovitz."

I shuddered. "You can have them both."

"I'd always thought that slivovitz was about the worst drink I ever tasted," the Wing Commander said. He took his coat off because it was warm there in the sun, and I gave his left chest a double take. He was wearing both the D.F.C. and the D.S.O.—both with bars.

"You got pretty ribbons," I said, and then added, hastily, as he was about to speak, "I know —in your squadron they give them out whenever

56

you buy a tin of sardines." That's what they all say.

He smiled ruefully. "Right, old boy."

"I know a worse drink than either grappa or slivovitz," I said, and they looked startled. "That kümmel you get in London. On the bottle it says 'made temporarily in the United Kingdom.' Be sure and pass it up. I think it's the reason for the petrol shortage."

"It would be a treat to be in New York just for a week," the Wing Commander said. "My God, think of a week in New York! No blackout, all the beautiful food and drinks you wanted . . ."

"If this is a good show and there's a real story in it, I'll be off to New York soon," I said, and they looked at me enviously.

"It'll be a big show all right," the Wing Commander said dryly. "Will you go to Hollywood when you get back?"

"If I can get someone to pay my fare out there," I said. "I mean if I can pick up some quick picture job."

"I was out there just before the war," the Wing Commander said reflectively. "A lot of nice people out there. Do you know Herbert Marshall?"

57

"My God," I sat up, startled. "He's the best friend I have in Hollywood."

"A good man—Bart," the Wing Commander said. "He's tried everything to get over here. He knocks himself out raising money for British War Relief and now he's selling bonds, but he still tries to get over here. One of our chaps just got back from Washington. He said that Bart went down there asking their help to get a visa. Our chap said to him, "After all, Mr. Marshall, you got half-killed in the last war serving in France. Do you want to lose the other half of your life in this war?"

"What did Marshall answer to that?" I asked, knowing damn well what Bart would answer.

"Marshall just said simply, 'Yes.' That Bart Marshall hates Germans," the Wing Commander said. "He's a hell of a citizen, and some people think he's just another film actor."

We talked of Marshall and of Nigel Bruce whom everyone calls Willie, and of Alfred Hitchcock whom everyone calls Hitch, and of Roland Young, whom everyone calls Charles Ruggles, and of Charlie Butterworth whom everyone calls Roland Young. I kept thinking of the last time I'd been in Hollywood some months before. I'd stayed with John McClain, as I always do, but we spent most of our time at Bart's. It was pleasant sitting there on the dock thinking about the really good guys I was lucky enough to know in Hollywood and elsewhere. The day I left Hollywood, Marshall had a party for me which was so much fun that it made me feel good here on a dock 6,000 miles from Hollywood. Jack Benny and Ronnie Coleman and Roland Young and Walter Duranty and Bill Powell were there and Adolph Menjou, taking a drink after six years of enforced abstinence caused by ulcers, was there too. I'd just come from Russia, and there was Charlie Butterworth and Charlie Einfeld and Charles Boyer and the rest of my friends, and they kept asking me about Russia. I couldn't answer one of their questions.

"I was only in Russia three months," I confessed weakly, "and I left knowing no more about Russia than when I went there."

Walter Duranty chuckled at that. "Hell, I lived in Russia for twenty years, and when I left I didn't know much more about it than when I first went there."

Boyer never said a word. He just sat there at Marshall's bar with a self-satisfied smile on his face. He looked as though he felt apart from everyone in the room, although everyone there was a friend of his. Boyer looked as though he'd just won the Irish Sweepstakes and had been told that there's to be no income tax on it.

"This is the happiest day of my life," Boyer said, when I asked him what was with him.

"So?"

Boyer talks slowly and he has that same suggestion of French accent that he has in pictures. He's a well-liked man—Boyer. By now Bart's wife, Lee (the only girl allowed at the party), was bartending and she was so happy because the usually abstemious Boyer had asked for another drink.

"Whatever are you celebrating, Charles?" she asked curiously.

"I will tell you," he said, smiling like a kid who is revealing a terrific secret. "I will tell you why this is a happy day for me. Today I became an American citizen. You understand—I am an American citizen. Is that not something to celebrate about? It is nothing, perhaps, to the rest of you. It is something very tremendous to me. Mind you, though, I still love France, as much as I ever did."

I thought of all this sitting there on the dock

60

and the Wing Commander and the British Major talked and the words flowed easily and casually over me because by now I'd put my knapsack under my head and, using it as a pillow, had stretched out, and life was good. I kept thinking of that afternoon and remembered how we'd all toasted Boyer and how happily embarrassed he had been. It sometimes takes a naturalized American to remind the rest of us of the heritage we and we alone enjoy.

The thoughts I had lying there in the sun on a dock in the Portsmouth Naval Yard are a part of the great event that was to take place, and, when I think of that event, I remembered that pleasant hour on the dock with the Wing Commander and the British Major, and they are indivisible from what happened during the next twenty-four hours.

"I guess I'm the only one in the world who really liked Hollywood," I said out loud. "I never worked there and if you don't work there, and only stay for short stretches, it's fun."

We were joined at that point by a Canadian Captain—a press officer. He introduced himself and told us that it was about time we left. He asked us what ships we had been assigned to

61

and the Wing Commander and the British Major said they'd been assigned to the destroyer *Berkeley*.*

"Your American, Colonel Hillsinger, is also on the *Berkeley*," the Canadian said. "I assume that you are too?"

I said no, I was assigned to the *Calpe*, but I wished he could fix it so I could be on the *Berkeley*. I didn't know anyone who was to be on the *Calpe*, and I'd rather be with Colonel Hillsinger and my two companions on the *Berkeley*. The Canadian press officer shook his head. "If the C.C.O. put you on the *Calpe*, well, you go on the *Calpe*."

"How come a Canadian press officer is on the show?" I asked.

He smiled. "It's pretty much of a Canadian show. You'll learn all about it when you get aboard the *Calpe*. But I can tell you that our generals got awfully tired of having our Canadians sit on their fannies these past two years. So did the troops themselves. Anyhow, they insisted

*When the *Berkeley* received a direct hit at Dieppe, both the Wing Commander and the Major were killed, and, because their names have not as yet been released, I cannot identify them. Colonel Hillsinger was seriously injured. His leg was blown off but he recovered. He has been awarded the D.S.C. and the Order of the Purple Heart.

that they go on the next big do and this is it. Our men want to fight. You should have heard them this morning when Ham Roberts talked to them."

I'd heard of General James Roberts. General McNaughton was the C. in C. of the Canadian forces—Roberts his divisional commander. I knew that the troops thought highly of him. He had been born in Titestone, Manitoba, and educated at Edsom College in England. He had gone through the Canadian Royal Military College at Kingston (Canada's West Point) and had served as a gunner in France until wounded in March, 1918. A fighting general, they called Roberts. I mentioned this to the Canadian press officer.

"I'll say he is. You should have heard him talk to our lads this morning. Of course they all had been told that they were off on maneuvers in which they were to use live ammunition. Once they were aboard the ships, Roberts told them that this was to be no picnic—it was the real thing. You should have heard them yell. They're really rarin' to go. He told them that they were to cross the Channel—they won't know exactly where they're going until the ships pull out—and he told them that the toughest part of the trip

63

would be going through a German mine field about three quarters of the way across the Channel. They've laid a ten-mile mine field which is too long to go around. We've got to go through it. Roberts told them that and then he added, 'But I want you men to know that your General will be first through the mine field, and if I get through safely so will all of you.'"

"Pretty good," I said. "He must have plenty of guts."

"He has," the press officer said, shaking his head admiringly. "His destroyer goes through first, and it has a hell of a chance to get blown up. And now we're off. I have a car for you gentlemen who are to be on the *Berkeley* and one for you to take you to the *Calpe*."

We shook hands and said cheery good-byes and I climbed into a car and headed for the *Calpe*. She was a destroyer of the Hunt class. There are a dozen or so destroyers all named after famous British hunts. The *Berkeley* was one. So was the *Calpe*. It always seemed rather silly to me to name a destroyer after what amounted to a country-club fox hunt, but then lots of things in Britain seem silly to me just as I am sure lots of things in America seem silly to visiting Britons. We're about even on that score. The *Calpe* looked very small and tired, but all destroyers look tired in their war paint. I climbed up the gangway and there was a good-looking young man in the uniform of a naval lieutenant waiting there.

"Your identification?" he asked, smiling. I gravely handed him my papers, and he introduced himself as Lieutenant Boyle, attached to the staff of Captain J. Hughes-Hallett of Combined Operations.

"Shall we go to the wardroom?" he suggested, and we did. It is almost a rite on British war ships that a visitor is first given the courtesy of the ship by the offer of a drink. There were several men sitting in the wardroom and I looked at them with curiosity. Everyone there was a stranger to me, yet I knew before long I'd know them all. Boyle ordered a drink for me, tea for himself.

"Technically, I suppose I'm a member of the forces now, Right?"

Boyle, puzzled, said that was right.

"In which case," I said, "I will be allowed to buy a drink. I've never been allowed to buy a drink on any of His Majesty's ships. It will be a change."

The little steward broke in, "Right, sir. In addition to the crew, we will have perhaps another sixty or seventy officers aboard and you all have the privilege of signing for drinks."

"Sixty or seventy extra? Where will we all sleep?"

The steward smiled. "I'm afraid sleeping will be out of the question, sir."

Boyle laughed too. "As soon as we leave shore I'll give you the whole plan. I've been assigned to take care of you. When you hear the plan I don't think you'll want to sleep. Should be a very interesting show from your point of view. This is the headquarters ship. The whole do will be run from here."

The wardroom reverberated with vague off-stage mutterings and groanings, and then sharp commands barked from the deck drifted down the hatchways to us. The ship shook herself like a puppy which had just come out of the water and, "We're off," Boyle said calmly. "Now first of all I want to introduce you to the General. He asked me to bring you up to see him as soon as we shoved off."

We climbed up two sets of iron ladders to the top deck. There was a fairly large, pleasant enough room there and Boyle led me in. A table had been set up and three men were doing things with radio instruments and head phones. But I didn't notice that. My eyes were on the big smiling man who stood up as I entered. His mustache was dark and closely cropped. His graying hair added a note of distinction to an already fine firm face. "Grizzled," was the word for the General.

"Glad you're on board," he said genially. "I'm Roberts."

"Glad to know you, sir," I said, weakly. What was it the Canadian press officer had repeated? ". . . but I want you men to know that your General will be first through the mine fields, and if I get through safely so will all of you."

"This is lovely, oh, just lovely," I said to myself, only half listening to Roberts. The charm of being the first to go through a mine field completely evaded me for the moment. For what? For a lousy story! I should have stood in bed indeed.

". . . so this room will be our headquarters," Roberts was saying. "Meet Air Commodore Cole.* He's our liaison with the RAF for the show. We're apt to be pretty busy once we get

*A few hours later Air Commodore Cole was seriously wounded. He was awarded the D.S.O. for gallantry under fire.

into action, but feel free to come in when you wish. You've been well vetted," he smiled, "and I've been told that we don't have to keep anything from you. Have you been told the plan yet?"

"I was about to brief him, sir," Boyle said.

"Good. Then I'll see you later, and if there's anything you want to know, don't hesitate to ask." General Roberts nodded and Boyle and I left. We climbed down the ladders again. We sat at a table and young Boyle took out some maps.

"We are headed for Dieppe," he said. "Of course, we have a mine field to get through first, and we'll probably get our heads blown off there," he added cheerfully, "and never reach Dieppe. Still . . . "

"You make it all sound very interesting," I said, politely. "You don't mind if we have a drink while you tell me more?"

He didn't, so I ordered one tea, one whisky.

4

W E ARE headed for Dieppe," Boyle repeated. "There are several objectives there we are after and which we will get. Always providing," he added smiling, "that we don't get our heads blown off going through that damn mine field."

"Why not forget about the mine field? It's being swept, isn't it?"

He nodded, "But those mine sweepers don't get them all. And of course they're doing this

69

one in a hurry. In fact they're sweeping it now. Dieppe," he added unexpectedly, "used to be a great place for honeymoon couples."

I knew that. I knew too that when the secretaries of London brokers became fed up with Brighton, they'd persuade their bosses to take them to Dieppe. Dieppe was a sort of poor man's Monte Carlo. It had a Casino. I remember Bill Corum, the New York sports writer, telling me how he landed at Dieppe in 1918 with his regiment. The first thing they saw was the Casino, and Corum fell in love with France on the spot. That night he hurried to it but was horrified to find that the Casino had been turned into a hospital. This, to Corum, as to any other man who likes an occasional whirl with the wheel seemed to be sacrilege.

"Ever been to Dieppe?" young Boyle asked curiously.

"Two weeks ago," I told him nonchalantly, and his eyes popped out.

"How was that?" he gasped.

"With the night fighters. I flew with them one night and we went over Dieppe."

"You actually flew in combat with them?" the kid was really excited. "I've often wanted to do that. Tell me about it."

70

"Nothing happened," I said ruefully. But I told him about it anyhow. It is a night I won't forget for a long time. It was exciting without being dangerous. The quiet sounds a ship makes going half speed crept into the wardroom. I told him all about it and although the story of it hardly figures in the actual raid it might be worth repeating here.

For nearly a year I'd been after a trip with the night fighters and finally the Air Ministry had arranged it. I was to proceed to an airdrome in Kent where two crack squadrons of "intruders" were stationed. An "intruder" is an offensive night fighter. He goes looking for trouble. This group used the two-motored Douglas Boston which our army calls the A-20A. It is a beautiful aircraft, perfectly fitted for this difficult job as bomber-fighter. "Intruders" flew high over France and Holland, looking for enemy airports. When they locate one they hover over it, waiting for German bombers to return from sorties over Britain. Then they give the bombers hell. They use a neat trick which sometimes works. They try to figure out what color landing lights the Germans are using on the particular night and they show these lights. If they guess right (the

71

Germans change the color nightly) they are all
right. If they guess wrong they get a dose of
flak and lots of attention from German fighter
aircraft. Sometimes they don't bother showing
lights. They just dive down and "beat up" the
airdrome—to use the RAF phrase. They carry
light bombs and plenty of machine guns and
cannon. It is dangerous but exhilarating work,
and the pilots are all specially trained for the
job. This airdrome was a particularly fine one
and the pilots a great bunch. They were a bit
more mature than the usual RAF squadron;
their average age was about twenty-four. Their
quarters were about a mile from the airdrome—
a lovely old red-brick house which had been a
school. When I arrived, the young Commanding
Officer showed me my room.

"We are very hospitable here," he said gravely.
"As you can see by the sign, we want to make
our guests happy."

I looked at a white card tacked under the bell.
The card read, "If you want a mistress during
the night, ring twice." This was an act of startling
hospitality I had never been offered at any other
RAF station before, but the C.O. laughingly ex-

72

plained that this had been a girls' school and in pedagogical language "mistress" meant teacher. They had never bothered to remove the signs in the bedrooms; in fact, they were very proud of them.

When night came we drove to the airport where I was fitted with bulky flying clothes and a parachute. My pilot was Squadron Leader Farqueson-Smith, and he had laughing eyes and a long handlebar mustache of which he was very proud.

"Longest mustache in the RAF," he boasted. His ribbons showed that his preoccupation with hirsute frivolities did not hamper his ability as a flyer. He was twenty-five and he had both the D.S.O. and D.F.C. So far he had gotten fifteen German planes and in addition had beaten up innumerable airports. Just as shadows began to engulf the field we walked to his aircraft and he explained about the parachute and the rubber dinghy.

"You are to sit in the nose," he said. "You can see everything from there. Now, in case you have to bail out—not that I expect you'll have to— there are a lot of things to remember. First you slide back the grating on the floor of the nose.

73

Then you drop through it. Of course that opening was probably made for Shirley Temple, and I doubt if you'll be able to make it. I'm just giving you the form. After you drop out, reach with your right hand for this handle and pull it. Not too hard or you'll pull the bloody thing off and your chute won't open. When you land in the water, grab this handle to your right and pull that. There is your rubber dinghy. Unbuckle the harness of your parachute. Get rid of it as soon as possible, because the whole thing is pretty heavy and is apt to pull you down. Then get out of your heavy flying clothes. And wait. Just wait a few days and maybe you'll be picked up."

I climbed into the nose with great difficulty. The whole thing fitted a bit snugly around the hips. I put my helmet on and plugged a cable into a socket. Now I could talk to the pilot who was behind and above me. The helmet was fitted with a metal disk which hit my mouth and which enabled me to talk to the pilot easily. He warmed up his motors. It was hot there in the glass nose and the heavy parachute harness was confining. I knew I'd never have nerve enough to jump anyway and, if I did, I'd never remember all the things one had to do to make the damn thing open

74

—so I slipped out of the heavy gear and felt much more comfortable.

The pilot called, "Everything all right?"

"Everything lovely," I said.

"We'll take a flip over the Channel," he said. "You can talk to me any time you wish. Hold your hats, kids, here we come."

We rushed down the black concrete runway. The nose lowered and for a nerve-wrecking split second I thought the nose was going to hit the ground, but that was only because here in front of the motors, virtually in front and ahead of the airplane, I was getting a different perspective than I'd ever had before. And then we were in the air. He rose sharply, circled once and headed for the Channel only a few miles away.

The moon high over the Channel was an orange ball, occasionally veiled by swirling white wisps of cloud. We were flying low and could see that the Channel tonight had a smooth, placid surface. In the glass-enclosed nose, sitting ahead of the motors, their roar came through the glass, muffled and dimmed, no louder than the droning of a fly. You feel very much alone up there in front, with the night on either side of you, with the sky above and the water below. I hoped, too,

75

that the glass was as strong as the pilot said it
was.

"It's so strong you can't even kick a hole in it,"
he had told me cheerfully before we started on
this night flight.The fast Boston A-20A hurried
toward France and enemy territory. This is one
of the loveliest aircraft ever to be born on the
blueprints of an American factory. Laden as
we were with bombs and with plenty of ammunition for our guns, the speed indicator in front
of me showed 280 miles an hour. We had 3,200
horses pulling us; each motor was 1,600 horse-
power, and both were singing sweetly.

Then clouds left the moon alone for a moment,
and ahead I could see a thin pencil line on the
horizon. It grew, and then the jagged cliffs of the
French coast, ghostly in the yellow moonlight,
appeared. We stayed low becouse if you are low
enough the curvature of the earth prevents radio
location. Even the fine ears of the German radio
detectors couldn't pick us up when we were
flying "wave high," as the pilots call it. We climbed
a bit now and swung along and over the coast.
There was nothing real about this. No light
showed in the miniature towns below. This pilot
knew the danger spots, and he was apparently

76

avoiding them, for no streaks of red flak came up
at us. Then we saw a thin, winding strip of quick-
silver and the pilot called cheerfully. "That's the
Somme." I was flying over land of rather bitter
memory. In late June, 1940, I was sitting in the
Ritz bar in Paris, listening to nitwits who kept
saying complacently, *"Ils n'auront pas Paris. Ils
ne passeront pas le Somme."* We heard it all over
Paris in those days. We heard it from everyone
except General Horace Fuller, then military
attaché at the American Embassy, the most brilliant military strategist I have ever met in half
a dozen warring countries. But we never believed
Fuller. The French had stopped the Germans once
in another war at the Somme. Now? "Waiter,
another Pernod—they'll never take Paris. They'll
never cross the Somme."

When we foreign correspondents stop being
reporters and become prophets, we often become
as ridiculous as radio commentators and newspaper columnists in America who so blithely explain away the defeats of British and American
arms from a distance of 5,000 miles. We don't
do it often, and there are men in London like
Raymond Daniell of the *New York Times,* or Bill
Stoneman of the *Chicago Daily News,* or Ed

Beattie of the United Press whose records since the war began have shown that they have dealt only in fact, and never in fancy, and, therefore, have never had the humiliating experience of having their guesses come home to roost. But unlike them, I guessed once and I believed the cry of the Paris loafers—*"Ils n'auront pas Paris. Ils ne passeront pas le Somme."*

I thought of that, crossing the Somme, which only two years ago was sluggish and uneasy because of the weight of the French and British blood it carried. We swung to the west, and in the distance red and white streaks bisected the sky and I thought of Coney Island in 1918 when the lifeguards, including me, used to stay behind on Saturday night to watch the fireworks.

"That's Boulogne," the pilot chuckled through the intercommunication.

"Let's get closer," I yelled.

"No, chum," the pilot laughed. "Those pretty lights are very nasty flak, and they might bring us down. I don't mind you getting killed, but I have orders not to let you get captured. They might not treat you nicely."

We swung around and when the plane banked, I was alone again with a plate of glass between

78

me and the water a thousand feet below and there is no more lonely feeling. We swung north again over the Channel, and it was calm and quiet, and the fireworks over Boulogne were in back of us and a thought came into my glass-enclosed chamber, and the thought was this: "The pilot and that rear gunner holding his gun button tensely do this every night, and it's business with them, and every night some of their pals get killed doing this, and they must feel a bit resentful merely acting as pilot and protector to a reporter just here for the ride."

"That's Dieppe to the left," the pilot called through his speaker, much as a London guide would say, "And on our left we have the Houses of Parliament, and you'll notice that the famous roof built by William Rufus in 1200 is no longer there. It was destroyed by fire May 10, 1941, and here, on the right . . . "

"Dee-epp." I repeated. I always wondered how to pronounce the name of that place. Dieppe was a line of cliffs, milk-white in the moonlight. Behind the cliffs were dark blobs, and I wondered which was the Casino and I wondered whether German officers were down there playing roulette. And we had flashed by Dieppe before their guns had

79

even a chance to fire. I never thought I'd be on my way there within two weeks.

In peacetime, boats went from Newhaven, on Britain's south coast, to Dieppe, and they advertised: "Only sixty-seven miles." When you were fed up with Brighton—Atlantic City is our equivalent to Brighton—you'd drive over to the nearby Newhaven and hop an overnight boat to the playground on this part of the French coast. The trip was five dollars.

We swung out into the Channel again, and the moonlight danced impudently on the most important body of water in the world, and you wondered why everything appeared so peaceful. By now, through familiarity, my glass enclosure seemed safe and secure, and I reached out and punched the heavy glass and leaned forward, finally lying down so that I was looking directly ahead and downward, watching the tiny white-caps born of a sudden breeze dance merrily on the surface. It was good to know that we were flashing at almost 300 miles an hour across the English Channel toward Churchill's island on a magic carpet from my own country. The longer you live abroad, the more American you get and the prouder you get of American institutions and

80

of American industry which could produce something like this Douglas Boston, which kept singing evenly, serenely, as though to say, "Don't worry—I won't let you down."

"Is that lighthouse flashing?" I called through the intercom.

"No lighthouses out here," the pilot laughed. "This is the Channel."

I looked again, and still thought I saw a light. The clouds, tired of flirting with the moon, had come low now to play hide-and-seek with the whitecaps, but through them I saw a pinprick of light. It was a light that fluttered irregularly like the heartbeat of a tired bird; a light that flickered, then died away only to be reborn when the ghostly white clouds swirled away. The airplane lurched to the right as the pilot banked.

"It is a light," came through the earphone. "You're right. No lighthouse. It's flashing—my God, he's flashing S O S!"

We circled low. But a sudden Channel mist made it hard to see anything. We circled, and occasionally in the exact center of our circle the light flashed, hopefully now, it seemed.

"Angel calling, Angel calling." The pilot's voice wasn't gay and laughing now. He was calling his

81

airdrome. It sounded like a Hollywood war picture. "Are you receiving, over over?"

The voice broke in, "Ronny calling. Receiving you clearly, receiving you clearly. Over over." And then my pilot saying, "Angel calling. Take position fix. Have you position fix? Returning now over." And again, "Receiving you clearly. Have position fix. Are you returning now? Why do you wish position fix? Over." My pilot, a bit petulant, "Never mind, never mind. Returning immediately."

The wing, which had dropped while we circled, rose and now the slight hum of the motors increased and the speed indicator read 290 again, but inside my glass case it was still fairly quiet, and yet even there I could feel the tension of what I didn't know. We straightened out now—"flat out" as the pilots say—and the pilot told me, "That's one of our chaps, you know. Probably a fighter pilot who bailed out this afternoon. He's in his rubber dinghy and luckily his torch had strong batteries. He's about fifteen miles off Brighton. We'll drop back to the airport and tell them about it. They'll have a boat out in no time."

The British coast, curly breakers meeting white sand, flashed below us.

"That's Brighton," the pilot called. We flew for ten minutes, then circled, and I knew we were over the airdrome. Then a thin triangle of light appeared below us.

"That's home," the pilot chuckled. "If there are Huns about, we don't show lights at all. Got to pray your way in then." I looked at our wing tips and magically a colored light had appeared on the tip of each to tell the ground crew we were friends. We landed nicely and now the pilot, knowing that no German ears could listen to his local intercommunication, talked freely to the operations room of the airdrome.

"Did you get my fix?" he asked. "Got the position right? Good. Found a chap out there signaling S O S. One of ours, I imagine. Okay. Right. Have him picked up."

The pilot turned his attention to me. "Want to see London from the air?" I definitely wanted to see London from the air, and the slim Boston began to dance down the runway. We skimmed along the black concrete, and what if there wasn't a light to show us the way? The sure-handed pilot, his fingers featherlight on the stick, knew that runway and so did this lovely aircraft. He pulled the stick back and we rose surely, clearly, gracefully, and you could feel somehow that this plane was as honest and as trustworthy as the men who had sweated to produce it. We cut diagonally through the night, away from the earth beneath, and the needle on my altimeter leaped up to two, then three thousand feet within what seemed to be seconds.

"We're at 5,000 feet now," the pilot called. "She climbs fast."

"Made in America, sweetheart," I told him, complacently, and then, relenting, "but you handle her well. You must have been taking lessons by mail."

"Used to give them before the war," he said calmly. "Gave 3,000 hours' worth of lessons. We've got to keep above those balloons over London. They're very dangerous."

"I hear those balloons got two Heinkels and a Hurricane last week," I told him, and then he said that we were on the outskirts of London. I lay down, by now trustful of the glass, and peered below. We were at 7,000 feet and it was chilly.

"We're over Hammersmith. We're approaching Kensington and we're over the West End. Recognize it?" His voice sounded like that of Ted Husing or Clem McCarthy announcing the running of the Kentucky Derby. It was 3 A.M. and London was asleep. From here not a sign of light showed in London. London might have been dead, but I knew that the night had a thousand eyes in London, and that those thousand mechanical eyes were on us. By now they'd received messages saying that we were friendly intruders. But I knew that a thousand fingers of gun crews were itching down there below. Usually a plane over London means a German plane, and it's always open season for such game.

We flashed over where I knew the Houses of Parliament to be, but from that height we couldn't see them, and I realized how absurd were the claims of Hun bombers that they had only aimed at targets over London. Even on a reasonably clear night such as this you could only find targets by instruments—not by your vision, as they boasted.

We flew up the Thames, and although I could not distinguish one building on the Embankment from another, I knew now from the bridges we crossed that we were over the Savoy Hotel. I felt a pang of remorse coming, knowing that the roar of our motors in the still night air would wake

85

a hundred people down there in my hotel. It had happened to me dozens of times, and when the sound of a plane wakes you in the bleak hours of the night you awake to a strange, unnatural world. Your subconscious mind, after two years of believing that all planes heard late at night are enemy planes, cries "danger coming," and your half-numbed conscious mind in vain answers, "There hasn't been any alarm." But in this fight, your subconscious usually wins because even your conscious mind knows that you have often slept through sirens and awakened only to the sound of enemy airplane motors above or of exploding bombs below.

We were north a bit now, and the clouds parted to show the placid dome of St. Paul's Cathedral, guarding the city as it has guarded it in a hundred raids. Beyond St. Paul's was Fleet Street and I could imagine the men in newspaper offices looking up, wondering thoughtfully if this was a jerry plane the radio detectors had missed. Sometimes they don't sound sirens for a single enemy plane. I could imagine Christiansen, editor of the *Express*, down there, just putting his paper to bed, and Percy Cudlipp, editor of the *Herald*, frowning because the sound of our motors inter-

86

rupted him as he wrote his final editorial. I could
imagine Michael Foot of the *Evening Standard*
making up his first edition, and Gerald Barry of
the *News Chronicle* swearing mildly because our
plane had disturbed his train of thought. I'd be
to blame if editorials were bad tomorrow. But
not only Fleet Street and the correspondents of
the American morning papers and American news
services were awake down there below in that
sprawling dark city, where not a light showed.
They and twenty thousand ARP wardens and
fire watchers and ambulance drivers and firemen
were awake. The city slept, but she slept well-
guarded now at 4 A.M. Then in the east a very
thin ribbon of light showed, and my pilot called:
"Time for breakfast, chum," and we circled away
from London and headed for our airport seventy
miles away.

Like a good horse hurrying home to the barn
for its oats, our Boston stepped out, now seeming
to know that the long night's vigil was done. An
early dawn was lifting the night from the airport
as we circled over it. We landed lightly, sure-
footedly, and the plane swung docilely to its position on the field. I slid back the gadget you bail
out through if things go bad, and shook the stiff-

ness out of my legs. The pilot, looking like a man from Mars in his odd helmet, his intercommunication mask hiding his face, his harness and his parachute, climbed down, smiling.

"Bacon and eggs now," he suggested. "And a spot of beer. Sound good?"

"Sounds good," I admitted. "How about that kid in the Channel? Can we find out if he was picked up all right?"

"Oh, I guess they got him all right," he said casually. "Anyhow, we did what we could."

Life and death are casual matters to these RAF pilots because they deal in them every night. It wouldn't do to worry about one lone pilot out there in the Channel. It wouldn't do to wonder whether or not rescue boats had found him or whether he was still floating out there on his tiny raft, despairingly flashing his small light while strength remained. He'd been shot down, probably wounded, and by now if he hadn't been picked up he'd be weak and discouraged.

"No, let's not find out," the pilot said. "If we learn they couldn't find him it'll only make us feel bad." We walked over to the mess, talking about Nat Gubbins' funny column in the *Sunday Express*; talking about the poor Scotch we got

88

in London; talking about how good the blackout was over the capital; talking of the golden morning which had so unobtrusively and softly crept over the airdrome during the past few moments.

He was right. It would be better not to know.

This is the story I told young Boyle, sitting there in the wardroom. "Those pilots are marvelous," he said admiringly. "And such kids—most of them."

"How old are you?" I asked, amused.

Boyle colored slightly. "I'll be twenty-one in about three hours. Tomorrow is my twenty-first birthday."

A sailor stuck his head into the room. "Captain Hughes-Hallett would like to see you on the bridge, sir."

Apparently the real show was about due to start. Boyle and I climbed up three sets of iron ladders and found the bridge.

5

CAPTAIN J. HUGHES-HALLETT was sharp featured, keen-looking. He was in charge of the naval operations in connection with the raid. He would be complete boss until we arrived at Dieppe. Then General Roberts would take over in conjunction with Air Commodore Cole. Combined Operations meant exactly that —the army and navy and the air force acted as a team in perfect harmony.

"A bit crowded up here, I'm afraid," Hughes-

Hallett said, apologetically. "In fact, our whole ship is a bit crowded. I'm afraid once we get into combat there won't be much room up here for you. But you have the run of the ship. Just try not to get in the way," he added, smilingly taking the sting out of his words. "Every man on board has a job to do. You realize that, I know."

We were lying about two miles off shore and this apparently was our rendezvous point. There was no moon as yet, and it was quite dark. The Channel was being kind to us; the water was calm and friendly-looking. Hughes-Hallett had the difficult job of getting all of the ships which were to accompany us in line and getting them away together. We could see ships all around us. By now, all wireless communication had stopped. It would be "radio silence" from now on. A man with a blinker light stood beside Hughes-Hallett, and when the captain barked sharp orders the light blinked quickly.

"This is rather a historic occasion," Hughes-Hallett turned to me. "This is the greatest invasion of its kind ever attempted in modern warfare. We have every type of smaller ship with us from transports to small motor-torpedo boats."

Ships stretched as far as the eye could pierce

the gloom. There were fat transports, heavy bellied, with the small invasion barges which were on their decks behind protruding coverings of protective burlap. There were the long tank landing craft, low in the water, and occasionally the sleek form of a destroyer slithered by on its way to her post.

"That's *Jennifer* there on the port side." Hughes-Hallett seemed to be talking to himself. "Bit close . . . Tell her to shift a bit . . . Have *Ajax* come up closer . . . What the devil is *Leicester* doing there? She knows where she should be . . . Tell her . . . "

The light blinked and ships moved to port and starboard. Now and then the throaty rumble of a motor-torpedo boat would cut through the thousand small sounds which the night seemed to muffle—sounds of engines, sounds of commands being given and always the thin lapping of the waves against the steel hull. A ship has sounds of her own. When it rolls even slightly she groans a bit and creaks in protest. Steam panted easily from the funnel of our destroyer as though the ship was breathing. There were eight men on the small bridge.

92

"Any cruisers or battle wagons with us?" I asked Hughes-Hallett.

He shook his head. "We have destroyers with us, but nothing larger. This isn't it, you know," he added dryly.

For months we had all been considering the project of a so-called second front. That was the big operation we knew would come eventually and it had become "it" to us.

"Still, this is the biggest thing we've tried so far," Hughes-Hallett said.

"There'll be a lot of aircraft engaged, won't there?" I asked.

He nodded. "Yes. Every available fighter aircraft."

That I knew. The week before I'd spent two days with Air Marshal Sir Sholto Douglas, C. in C. of RAF Fighter Command. He had gone to Southampton to inspect a new RAF set-up there and had invited me along. I had told him that I hoped to go on the next raid and Sir Sholto had become very serious.

"It'll be a big show," he had said soberly. "Naturally you can't ask me anything about it but I'm a little worried. Not worried about the success of it. The planning has been too careful.

But I am worrying about the casualties—my casualties. We've got to maintain an umbrella of fighters, and I know some of them are going to be lost. In fact, I expect to lose 100 fighters, and that isn't a pleasant thought."

"You can't do anything without expecting casualties," I suggested, rather inanely.

"I know. I know," he had said. "But I don't like to think of it. I know most of my fighter boys. You know a lot of them. It isn't a pleasant feeling to know that many of them are going to get it."

That was all. Men like Sir Sholto Douglas never volunteer vital information even to men they trust—unless they are concerned directly in the operation. War teaches one the value of reticence if it does nothing else. During war, confidences even among friends are not easily given, nor easily broken. All Sir Sholto had told me with those few words was that the next raid was to be a big one. However, it might have been months off and it might have been aimed at any place from Stavanger to Dakar for all the information he gave. Not that I was looking for information.

"Boyle will give you our schedule," Hughes-Hallett went on. "Our protecting aircraft arrive at dawn. We're quite on our own until then. I

94

think they should protect us fairly well once they arrive. We're a bit crowded now," he apologized again. "Do you mind? And be sure to wear your Mae West, especially when we go through that mine field."

I took the hint, and Boyle and I descended to the lower deck. Actually a destroyer has only one real deck, but there is a smaller deck above that and what it is called I don't know. We stood there for a while and then suddenly realized that we were off, and that a long line of shapes distinguishable only because they were darker than the water were following us. Then we went below to the wardroom again. Boyle spread out a map on the table. From a brief case he brought out several large photographs and put them in place.

"Here's a general view of Dieppe," he pointed to the map. "You'll notice various notations on it such as "Possible light gun" or "road block" or "anti-tank obstacle" or "house strengthened" and a hundred others. These all came from the RAF photos. They've been taking pictures of Dieppe and the country surrounding it for weeks; the last were taken yesterday. Take a look at them."

The photographs, of course, had been photostated. They looked as though they had been taken from a hundred feet up. Actually the amazing telescopic lenses used by the photographic section of the RAF could "see" from really terrific heights. Houses, block houses, road intersections, cliffs, occasional concrete pill boxes—all stood out boldly on the pictures. The information obtained from the photos had been used to make the military maps which all commanding officers would carry. The map itself was interesting. The key to it was in the upper left-hand corner. Some of it would make sense only to a military man.

"And here," Boyle added, "is our timetable."

He handed me three sheets of typed paper. Unfortunately I cannot reproduce it. As I read it I realized the weeks of work Mountbatten, Hughes-Hallett and Roberts had put in on it planning this raid. Because its publication would give the Germans a great deal of information as to how raids are planned (and will be planned in the future) Mountbatten's staff has quite wisely asked me not to use it. I can only say that every ten minutes something was scheduled to happen. To give one example, the zero hour was really 5:20. At that time landings would be made

96

on the beaches. But at 5:10 our eight destroyers
were to shell those beaches for ten minutes. Each
had its particular target. Even the number of
shells to be fired was there in the schedule. Exactly 1,780 shells were to be fired, and the three
beaches to be shelled were exactly 1,780 yards
long. That was typical of the schedule.

Reading it was like reading the script of an
exciting play. Reading it, you know it's going to
be a hit; the action is terrific, the dialogue marvelous. It's so good that you can't wait to see it
played. All of that absurd feeling of pessimism
I'd had the night before had left me. Now I could
laugh at it. I'd probably just been half-consciously
dramatizing myself. I'd been feeling sorry for
myself. I wasn't now. I was on my way to the
greatest opening night the world had seen for
years. I was the luckiest guy in the world, and
I felt ashamed of my ridiculous hunch of the
night before. This script was foolproof; it couldn't
miss. And what a show it would be! In addition
to the show I'd see, I even knew now what the
rest of the audience didn't know, and wouldn't
know. I knew all of the offstage directions. For
instance, I knew that at 11:30 in the morning,
two squadrons of Flying Fortresses escorted by

250 Spitfires would bomb the Abbeville airport. Abbeville was just thirty-nine miles in back of the city of Dieppe. It was the nearest airdrome to Dieppe. Bombing it with that pinprick bombing which, by virtue of the Norden bombsight, only our Fortresses are able to do, would keep German aircraft from refueling there. I knew now just what RAF squadrons would be up there fighting off the German bombers. That was a warming thought. There were no better pilots in the world than our Eagle Squadron kids. I hoped that Gussie Daymond and Peterson and Jimmy Dufours were getting plenty of sleep. Thinking of them I started to laugh and Boyle asked me what was the matter. I told him of how unhappy Sir Sholto Douglas was because those Eagle boys were being transferred to the American Air Force. Ever since Dec. 7th the Eagle Squadrons had wanted to transfer. They had made official application but nothing had happened. Then one afternoon six of them called on me at the Savoy. They were a delegation representing all three Eagle Squadrons. They told me that they'd tried everything but that they were as far away from joining the American forces as they'd ever been. Would I see what I could

98

do? Would I go to Sir Archibald Sinclair, Minister for Air, and ask him to release them? Would I go to Ambassador John Winant? Would I go to General Eisenhower? They wanted to get into American uniforms. Oh, they loved the RAF, but we were in the war now, weren't we? Then too the pay in the American air force was three times that of the RAF and, in addition, if you "bought it" the RAF had no pension plan; nothing but the RAF Benevolent Fund. Very earnestly they argued that though they'd love that extra pay their chief concern was in regard to the folks at home. Suppose they lost a leg or an arm—then what? No provision was made to take care of dependents of Americans in the RAF.

I was on a spot, all right. I knew that I had no right to even make a request of any of our military people. But the kids were so earnest and they had such faith in my ability to do something, that I had to try. I wrote to General Carl Spaatz, head of our air force. I apologized first for my presumption, but told him how close I was to the boys and how a year before I'd helped get the RAF to exempt them from paying income tax. Then I stated their case. Many of the Eagle boys were technically ineligible to join our forces because of physical limitations. There was Shorty, for instance, who lacked one inch of the American air force standard—but he'd made sixty daylight sweeps over France. Could this not be taken into consideration? I mailed the letter with feelings of trepidation. I knew Tooey Spaatz, but he would be quite justified in saying, "This is none of your business."

But he didn't. Instead, the phone rang at nine the next morning and the General's aide, Major Cy Bartlett, was speaking.

"The General got your letter," he said, "and he agrees with you a hundred percent. He has cabled Washington already asking permission to take over the Eagle Squadrons."

"He didn't think I had a hell of a nerve writing to him, did he?"

"No, he didn't," Bartlett said, "because he's not that kind of a guy. But I did . . . Anyhow you've gotten action, so tell the kids it's in the works."

I did. A few weeks later I was with Sir Sholto Douglas and he was in a gloomy mood. He talked about our Eagle boys and of how good they are. "And now," he said, "just when they're so well-trained that they are the equal of any fighter squadrons in the world, they are being taken

100

away from me. Yes, they're going over to Tooey Spaatz. General Spaatz is fine, excellent in every way, but I wish he'd let me keep those boys. I hate to lose men like Pete and Gussie and the rest."

"It certainly is tough," I said sympathetically, thanking the stars that Douglas didn't know my part in the transfer. And that's why I laughed when I knew the three squadrons would be with us at Dieppe. It would be just about their last big show before changing uniforms (and salaries).

"Entering the mine field," the little mess steward said laconically. "Better put on the Mae Wests and get on deck."

The life jackets which both the RAF pilots and the navy uses are called Mae Wests even in official language now. When they are inflated the reason for the name is very obvious. We slipped into the jackets the steward handed us and went on deck. There was just a fringe of moon but it cast no light at all. It was still calm, but now the calmness of the Channel seemed ominous. Back of us I could make out the bulky form of a ship, and I knew that many many more

101

were following. Then ahead of us and slightly to port I saw a light.

"The mine sweepers dropped lighted buoys where they had cleared," Boyle explained. "One about every half mile. We'll just try to pick those lights up and follow them."

We passed within twenty yards of the small green light and now we were in the mine field. We plowed along at rather a brisk pace and, looking over the rail, I could see the water churning to a white froth as we cut through it.

"We're really in no hurry, are we?" I asked Boyle. "Couldn't we take it easy through this mine field?"

Boyle laughed. "If you hit a mine going at twelve knots it has the same effect as if you hit one traveling at two knots."

Far ahead I saw another one of the small lights. So far so good. This would have been a beautiful time for the German planes to spot us. If they knew we were here now they could drop flares and make day out of the night. Then they could pick us off one by one. We couldn't dodge or zigzag because our margin of comparative safety was only about two hundred yards to either side of us. Once we tried escaping from bombs we'd

102

be right in the midst of the mines. You don't
actually have to hit a mine to get it. The Germans
lay acoustic and magnetic mines and if you get
close to them your ship just draws the mines to
her. General Roberts had been right when he
said that this would be the toughest part of the
whole operation.

Boyle had left and I stood there at the rail
alone. Our ship, sobered by the trip it was making,
seemed very subdued. The motors were only half
heard and not a voice broke the silence. It was
very dark and standing there I felt more alone
than I'd ever felt in my life. It was as though
the ship and I were the only ones in this part of
the world. We passed one more light.

A brisk breeze had sprung up, but I noticed
that I was sweating. I took off my coat, but that
didn't help. I peered ahead, looking for the next
buoy, but there was nothing ahead but darkness
and beyond that the enemy. The ship veered
slightly to starboard and I wondered in a panicky
moment if we had lost the trail left by the mine
sweepers. This was like an old-fashioned paper
chase, but perhaps not quite so much fun. The
darkness and the silence seemed to merge now
and become more oppressive. I couldn't even see

103

the form of the ship behind us, although I knew she wasn't more than a hundred yards astern. A sailor passed me and cursed half heartedly as he stumbled over a stanchion. It was comforting to hear even his throaty, "Bloody dark." I wasn't alone on this ship, after all. In fact somewhere below, above and around me were two hundred men, all, I hoped, equally as nervous as I. Now we veered to port and I was sure that we had lost the trail of the paper chase. And then suddenly a hundred yards away a tiny light showed; we were abreast of it and then we had passed it. One could breathe again and stop sweating. Always, in war, the suspense is more freightening than the actual combat. Suspense torments you by slow degrees; it is torture of the worst kind and it makes you weak and limp. Enough of it and panic grips you, warping your judgment and numbing the senses. On we went, hitting each little green light right on the nose. Hughes-Hallett was doing a masterful job up there on the bridge.

Then a bell clanged somewhere; voices still for nearly an hour were heard again; the ship seemed to breathe a sigh of relief. We were through the mine field and now, of course, you shrugged your

104

shoulders and told yourself that it hadn't been so bad after all. This was to tell your nerves to stop jumping, to tell your sweat glands that they had no need to work overtime now. We were through and now there was nothing ahead of us (we hoped) but some fifty miles of water. We were taking a much longer route than did the pre-war honeymooners on their sixty-seven mile Newhaven to Dieppe jaunts.

It was pleasant down in the wardroom. General Roberts was there with his two aides and with Air Commodore A. T. Cole, a lean and affable Australian. He was representing Air Marshal Leigh Mallory, who was in charge of the aerial part of the attack. The tension had gone, and we all had a drink and, except for the uniforms, this might have been the smoking room of a small ocean liner and we a group of business men on holiday. They were all congratulating the Air Commodore. It was he who had planned the path through the mine field. He had flown over the Channel several nights and had discovered the German mine layers dropping their eggs. Later he had observed German E boats going through the mine field and he had gotten an approximation of their path. Apparently he'd hit it just right.

105

Either that or our sweepers had done a very efficient job.

Roberts was not a General who stood too much on dignity. Like a good soldier he was relaxed now. Tomorrow would be a tough day, but to worry about it now would only be to borrow trouble. The entire plan was made. Now Roberts only had to carry it out and his part in the program would not begin until just before daybreak.

Roberts said unexpectedly, "I expect to go ashore about 8:30 if things are going according to plan. Like to join me?"

Would I like to join him? My only regret until now had been that I wasn't scheduled to land. But to actually set foot on enemy soil would be the best story of all. Would I like to join him?

"That is kind of you," I said gravely.

6

THE time for keeping secrets had passed, and now Roberts and Cole told me the whole story of the operation. They told me just how many men would land; how many Canadians; how many Commandos and how many Americans. Roberts went over the map with me, pointing out the two six-inch gun batteries the Germans had flanking Dieppe. These would be the objectives of the Commandos, and the whole success or failure of the raid would depend upon whether or not they did their job.

"Suppose everything goes according to plan," I asked, "and you are able to take and hold Dieppe? Is there any thought of establishing a permanent bridgehead? Are reserves and reinforcements ready to come over quickly to consolidate the position?"

"No," he smiled. "This definitely is not a second front. We have food, medical supplies, ammunition only for one day. This is a thrust, not a real offensive. We want, if possible, to realize our objectives, but actually more important is the fact that the raid will show the Hun that we are on the alert and on the offensive. It will show him that he can't relax his vigilance anywhere on the coast line; that he must, in fact, strengthen his defenses. He can only do that by withdrawing troops, planes, guns from Russia. We want him to know that we are apt to hit anywhere at any time."

"Then one of the primary objectives is to get them to withdraw troops from Russia?" I asked.

Roberts nodded. "Definitely. Anything we can do to ease pressure on Russia helps tremendously. Of course, we'd rather move in on a big scale and establish what people so foolishly call a "second front"; but you know as well as I do the

108

difficulties of that. Unfortunately," he added, smilingly, "the mass of our civilians and yours don't realize what the problem is, and they blame the British and the Americans and us Canadians for being dilatory."

I nodded agreement. "They've made a political question out of what is so obviously a military question."

Back in June (1942) I attended a few second-front meetings in Britain. They were held in places like Trafalgar Square, football parks and in large theaters in Manchester or Birmingham. The sincerity and honest intentions of the speakers and of the audiences were impressive. They wanted to help Russia, and only by establishing a second front in France could that be done on a large scale. Lord Beaverbrook led the second-front cheering section, and the Communist Party in Britain backed him up strongly. It was rather a strange alliance, but it was one in which both parties were in complete accord. I'd heard my Communist friends, Willie Gallagher, the M.P., Harry Pollitt, leader of the party, Ivor Montague, Ambassador Ivan Maisky and others voice telling arguments. The British Communists are not the long-haired, wild-eyed

creatures so often caricatured by American political cartoonists. No greater patriots exist in the
British Empire than Willie Gallagher or Harry
Pollitt. They were (and are) men who love their
country and who would sacrifice anything to help
win the war. I knew them all well and respected
them, as do even their political opponents. I had
returned from Russia some months before, full of
admiration and praise for the Russian people, and
I hadn't been backward about proclaiming and
writing what I thought of them. I had also written
and told how urgently the Russians needed our
help, and that the establishment of a second front
was apparently the most effective way of giving
them that help. We all knew that convoys, bound
for Russia, were getting an unmerciful beating,
and that the material which arrived there was but
a tiny drop in the bucket. I was as ardent a second-
fronter as anyone, to such an extent, that men
like Willie and Harry thought of me as a sort of
unofficial member of the party. Once I kidded
Willie Gallagher about why I liked Russia.

"Willie," I told him, "Russia is the only country
in the world where there is no communism."

"Ah, you just don't understand communism,"
Willie would answer in his thick Scottish accent,

110

and he was probably right. Your preconceived ideas of communism receive a terrific jolt when you go to Russia. What they have there is something so different from what the text books tell us communism is, that you end up quite bewildered. I know I did, but I was there only three months— long enough to get a slight glimpse into the hearts and minds of the people, but not long enough to even scrape the surface of understanding the present Russian political philosophy.

But it was impossible not to like and sympathize with men of the Gallagher, Pollitt and Montague type. In Britain, the second-front cry was by no means confined to members of the Communist Party. In addition to Beaverbrook, brilliant journalists like young Tom Driberg, Frank Owen, Michael Foot and the editors of most Fleet Street newspapers were ardent second-fronters. I thought I'd do an article for *Collier's*, blasting the British military and political leaders for their apparent lackadaisical tactics and, of course, including American military leaders in my condemnation. I went all around London asking just one question. "Why hasn't a second front been opened?" I only asked men who knew me well enough to realize they could talk off the record

111

without fear of being actually quoted. I talked to men like Averell Harriman, Ambassador Anthony Biddle and a few of the generals serving under Eisenhower. Eisenhower's generals are, I think, the best in the world. They are all young, vigorous, tough and aggressive. They are reticent about only one thing—they don't want their views printed. Trained to secrecy and discipline, they hate the thought of dramatizing themselves or of getting any personal publicity. I was lucky enough to get into a poker game with four of them one night. We talked about the problems involved in a frontal attack on France, while we drew to inside straights. Any reporter who plays poker with high-ranking officers knows damned well there is a rigid implication that everything said by them is off the record. That's why I can't name the generals or quote them. But they were unanimous in their views of an immediate second front. It just couldn't be done as yet. Not in France, anyhow.

I lost twenty pounds (eighty dollars) to those brilliant exponents of five-card stud and, when the game was over, they really felt a bit conscience-stricken about taking me so badly. I was the only civilian in the game, and they were afraid I'd think that they'd ganged up on me. But I told them that the lesson they gave me was well worth the eighty bucks.

"I'm probably the only reporter in Britain, who calls you four generals by your first names," I reminded them. "That's worth eighty dollars to *Collier's* and to me. And the lesson you gave me was well worth what I lost."

I never saw better poker players than those American generals. I was completely outclassed. Their strategy closely resembled military strategy. Occasionally, they would feint with a small pair and then withdraw, only to counter-attack vigorously again with three aces. Once you let them get off on an offensive, you had to retreat precipitously, or you'd get your brains knocked out. Often they would toss a smoke-screen of bluffing at you, and then, when you realized that this was merely a tentative "feeling-out" maneuver, you'd rush in, only to have the house fall on you—a full house. To most players, poker and drinking are synonymous. Our army officers have too much regard for the game to confuse it by adding whisky to its natural hazards. Among them, that night, I think the four generals knocked off about

113

six bottles of beer, which may, in part, explain their success.

This was in June, 1942, and these same generals were already laying plans for the offensive in Northern Africa; but not one of them even hinted that evening that anything of the kind was contemplated. Our generals know how to keep military secrets.

From them I went to A. V. Alexander (First Lord of the Admiralty), to Sir Sholto Douglas and to General Sir Hastings Ismay, who is known to one and all as Pug Ismay. I'd been to Russia with him some months before. I talked to men in the Air Ministry and, when I was all through, I had a pretty good picture of why a second front couldn't be attempted immediately. My second-front ardor died quickly. These men talked facts and figures. To them a second front was not a question of mere patriotism, of stirring crowds to emotional outbursts. It was a cold, military problem, involving men and machines of war—nothing else. I wrote a different story from the one I had planned and called it "Second Thoughts on a Second Front." When it appeared in *Collier's* I was panned unmercifully by left-wing friends both in Britain and America. I was com-

114

pletely bewildered by this criticism. I had written a factual story, telling just how strong the Germans were in France and what was needed to overcome this strength.

Every figure I gave had been the result of considerable research. Many of the figures I had been given I couldn't use because they would give information to the Germans. My Fleet Street pals looked at me suspiciously. After all these years had I gone over to the Tories? Was I just a blind follower of Churchill and his very, very, conservative group? In vain I protested that I was not writing any editorial but merely writing a factual article. Perhaps even now they think I went over to the "enemy." I'd like to quote some passages from the article. It is pertinent because it reveals the exact position of the German defenses in the summer of 1942. It tells why Dieppe was only a left jab slashed at the enemy instead of a terrific right-hand punch. I began:

"Billy Conn was doing very nicely. The thirteenth round had started, and he had Champion Joe Louis quite bewildered with the speed and cleverness of his attack. It looked as though there would be a new world's champion crowned within the next few moments. Conn only had to take it easy, keep on his feet, and the crown was his. But he was a throwback to the days of the

Fighting Irish; there is no neutrality in the soul of Pittsburgh's favorite son. He became bored with this dancing business.

"Conn's contempt for Louis grew, and then suddenly he started to trade punches with the fastest, most devastating puncher the world has ever known—and within a few brief moments young Billy lay on the floor, helpless, completely beaten. He had failed because he lacked the equipment to blitzkrieg Champion Joe. He had failed because for a brief moment he had tried to play Joe's game—and disaster was the inevitable result.

"Today, Britain is in the position that Billy Conn was in at the beginning of the thirteenth round. The RAF is slapping Germany silly. She is doing it by quick, daring thrusts by her airmen and her Commandos, working in co-operation with the navy. And today, eighty per cent of the people here on Churchill's Island and a great part of Russia and America are screaming to Britain: 'Stop boxing him! Go in and slug him!'

"In other words, Britain is being urged on all sides to establish a second front immediately, regardless of the German strength in France and other occupied countries. To date, Britain has been smarter than young Billy Conn. It is because Britain has had more experience than Conn in meeting terrific punches. She knows you can't swap punches with someone who carries heavier weapons than you do. And so, regretfully, she has had to forego the one thing which every pilot, every soldier, every naval man and every civilian in Britain so earnestly desires—a chance to land on the Continent and meet the enemy hand to hand.

"The thousands who are mounting soapboxes and

116

platforms in Britain, the hundreds who pen cutting editorials asking why the government does not start an immediate second front, the impatient Russians here in London and in Moscow quite understandably crying for vengeance against those who have killed some two million of their countrymen, the British civilian start-second-front-at-any-price brigade—forget that though the walls of Jericho crumbled at the blast of a trumpet, there is no reason to believe that the defensive walls of German Europe will fall at the blast of anything except superior guns, airplanes and tanks.

"Loud insistence upon the immediate opening of a second front has seemed to imply that Prime Minister Churchill and his government were not over-anxious to join with their Russian allies in an all-out effort on the Continent.

"Nothing could be further from the truth, of course, and the Molotoff agreements made in Washington have formally spiked that idea. Churchill talks privately as he does publicly, and no one who has ever heard his vituperative private comment in regard to the Germans, no one who has heard him express his admiration for the way the Russians have fought, would for a moment consider that Churchill is lukewarm on the subject of a second front. No one in Britain more earnestly desires to establish and maintain a bridgehead on the Continent than does Mr. Churchill.

"Nor would Churchill's worst enemies ever accuse him of cowardice or lack of decision when it comes to offensive action. He is a man who thinks in terms of attack. 'Defense' is a word that is repugnant to his aggressive nature. He has shown himself willing to gamble

117

on any occasion when there was a chance of winning the gamble. It is no secret that when Wavell attacked the Italians in the desert back in December, 1940, he bit off a little more than he could chew. He asked Churchill for more tanks. At that time, there was a serious threat of invasion in Britain, yet Churchill, without hesitating, sent Wavell the one armored division which Britain had, and with it the general smashed the Italian army thoroughly. This was typical of the chances which Churchill is willing to take.

"Not so long ago, he actually took weapons from the hands of soldiers here in Britain and sent those weapons to Russia. These were not surplus weapons; they were the only weapons the men had. Admittedly, Britain's army was weakened, but Churchill has shown more than once that he is committed wholly to the policy of putting weapons in the hands of those who are killing Germans.

"Why, then, has not this bold and aggressive leader ordered that a second front be opened? The answer is very simple. Such an undertaking is still a gamble. It may continue to be a gamble for at least another six or eight months. Any attempt to invade the Continent now might easily result in another and more costly Dunkirk. If those who have been leading the clamor for a second front knew what resources the German have in France, Norway and other possible invasion points, if they knew the vast amount of so-called 'special assault' equipment required, they would realize that their agitation was very, very premature.

"The British Intelligence has been very good to date. It has pipe lines which start deep in France and end up in the huge gloomy War Office in Whitehall. British Intelligence knows fairly accurately the German position across the Channel and realizes what difficulties must be overcome before any invasion is attempted.

"At least there are twenty German divisions in France —300,000 men. Several of these are armored divisions. For more than a year, this army has been preparing against invasion by a British army. Those who want a second front now point to the dramatic sorties made by the Commandos as proof that the defenses across the Channel are far from invulnerable. They point to the effectiveness of the storming of Saint-Nazaire, which suffered heavily at the hands of the Commandos. This is true, but the Germans have not neglected their defenses, and to date only raids of the Saint-Nazaire type have been able to penetrate them, and the casualties suffered by the British raiders were 73 per cent.

"There was once a little toy called the Maginot Line. It stretched from the Swiss border to Sedan, nearly seven hundred miles, and it bristled with guns. Small 37-mm. guns, larger 75s and 105s, the tremendous so-called 155 long, and the superheavy 220-mm. cannon. It will be recalled that very few of these guns were ever shot— except in practice. The Germans captured the Maginot Line by flanking it, and the Germans captured all of those guns. Today they are on guard against a British invasion. Today the whole coastal invasion area is manned by these excellent guns.

"They were not sent to Russia. RAF observers have seen them, have seen the new German Maginot Line which any British invasion force would have to smash. I have talked with these RAF observers, and they look

119

very thoughtful when they discuss the ground defenses they have seen, and the excellent anti-aircraft barrages which greet them when they are in the vicinity of such defenses.

"There is the problem, then—300,000 men, well equipped, well intrenched and with a rather large body of water protecting them. It is a military problem which has never been solved. Napoleon couldn't do it in 1802. The Germans couldn't solve a similar and much less difficult problem in July, 1940. Even then the Germans knew the difficulty of invading a country separated from you by water.

"Of course, had the Germans then tried to invade, they would have been successful. In July, 1940, Britain was suffering acutely from lack of equipment. There were less than 50 big guns in England then and only a handful of tanks. Had the German army, under the impetus of its own momentum, rolled across the Channel then, Hitler today would probably be eating his carrots and squash in the hotel in the Strand where I'm writing this article.

"But Hitler, who never flinches at German casualties, hesitated at the difficulties involved. He would have given a million men to take Britain. He thought that the operation would involve even greater losses. He made the mistake of overrating the British strength. Today the British and American leaders are not overrating his strength, but they have accurately gauged it.

"Let us consider what would be needed to establish a second front: To begin with, a primary rule of attack in warfare is first to pave the way with your artillery. In the last war, before any wholesale advance was at-

tempted, the artillery blasted away at the enemy, sometimes for days. This cardinal rule would have to be
violated in any attempted invasion of the Continent.

"The Channel is twenty miles across at its narrowest
point; in other places it is forty to one hundred miles
wide. You can't throw an artillery barrage at that distance. But you would have to weaken the enemy defenses somehow. Obviously the RAF would have to
serve as the artillery. They would have to bomb muni-
tions dumps and strafe the roads. They would have
to face a terrific resistance from land batteries and from
the splendid German fighters. The Beaufighters, the
Hurricanes, the Kittyhawk bombers, and the Bostons
would be the aircraft for this little job, as they are the
best low-flying bombers Britain has. The casualties would
be terrific. In low-flying attacks, they always are.

"A few weeks of this, and then we would have to
assume that the defenses had to some extent been weakened. Now comes the job of getting the infantry established. To begin with, it seems to be agreed that at
least thirty divisions would be needed. How would
these men be transported? Special assault barges would
be needed. At the moment there are not enough of
these in existence to move one division, much less thirty.
These would have to be barges which draw very little
water, so that they could glide over the heavily mined
Channel without encountering those nasty little floating
death pills. A fervent member of the second-front brigade
might ask: 'Why hasn't Britain these special assault
barges now, after nearly three years of war?'

"The answer is that, until recently, Britain had her
back to the wall, fighting for her very life. All of her

121

resources were concentrated in building weapons which would help her in that desperate defensive fight. She had to build destroyers, merchant ships, motor-torpedo boats, submarine chasers. Above all, she had to build ships to protect her life-line to Canada and America. She knew that eventually she would need these special assault barges, but she just didn't have the facilities to build them without neglecting more urgent needs.

"Men would also be sent by the hundreds in troop-carrying aircraft. Each of these aircraft can at best carry thirty men. How much ammunition, how many guns can thirty men carry? Not an awful lot.

"The second-fronters point hysterically to Rotterdam, which was taken by German troops who parachuted from aircraft—but they neglect to mention that Rotterdam was completely defenseless. They point to Crete, which was also taken by parachutists, but again neglect to mention that the defenders of Crete had absolutely no air protection and that their supplies had long since been cut off. It will be different dropping men in France. To begin with, the troop-carrying aircraft will be up against one of the greatest fighter planes yet devised by man, the German Focke-Wulf 190.

"Now, let us assume that we have landed our thirty divisions—say 450,000 men. Let's be charitable and only kill off a third of this number. We still have 300,000 men left. They have to be supplied with food and ammunition. They have to be supplied with heavy weapons to hold off the inevitable attack by tanks. The desert campaign has proved pretty well that, except in rare instances, the only way to beat tanks is with tanks.

"Now, an aircraft can do a lot, but it can't fly a twenty-

122

eight-ton General Grant tank to battle. The British could undoubtedly land a few by very large, specially made barges, but the mortality would be great. These barges would have to be screened by thousands of fighter and dive-bomber aircraft. The casualties among them would be very high. Once our invading army was established, it would have to be kept alive. It would be subject to a twenty-four-hour attack by German dive bombers. The German flares make day out of the blackest night now. Thousands of night fighters would have to be on the job constantly to guard against these skilled Hun dive-bombers.

"Meanwhile, our side wouldn't be able to harass the German tanks or artillery by dive bombing. We just have no dive-bombers at the moment—or, at least, none in quantity. 'Why not?' scream critics of the Churchill government. Once again, we must remember that the aircraft factories of Britain were strained to the utmost to produce the Hurricanes and Spitfires which won the Battle of Britain, the Wimpys, the Stirlings and the Manchesters, and the other heavy bombers which kept sniping away at German industrial centers. Britain did order dive-bombers from America in July, 1940, but, alas, they have not as yet materialized, except in small numbers.

"I've talked to air experts, and they agree that Britain would have to face a loss of from 1,200 to 1,500 aircraft a month if it were to give any adequate protection to an invading army on the Continent.

"There, rather briefly, is the problem of fighting on a second front. I've heard tired, worn-looking Commandos talk bitterly of the glib exponents of a second front.

123

"They won't have to be there," they say simply. "Why shouldn't they make speeches about it? Sure, we'll have a second front, but let's wait until we're ready."

"It must also be remembered that supplies do not come to Britain from America in such great quantities now. Enormous amounts of aircraft have been diverted to the Far East; thousands of guns and tanks have quite properly gone to Russia. And, during the past year, between four and five million tons of shipping have been sunk in the North Atlantic. Those glasses we've all been wearing are a bit too heavily rose-tinted. We may as well face it and admit that only the Russians have been doing any winning to date.

"There is, of course, one hopeful aspect. That is that the RAF has already established a second front. It is not at Calais or Boulogne, or at any invasion port. It is in the Ruhr, in Essen, in Cologne, in Lubeck, in a hundred industrial centers of Germany or German-occupied countries. Ever since the RAF began its monster raids on May 30th last, the Germans have felt the brunt of this second front. They have had to bring some aircraft back from the Russian front . . .

"There, to get back to where we began, is Billy Conn, smarter, more experienced, playing his own game, not a wide-open, slugging Billy Conn who is an easy target.

"Let those who shout loudest for the immediate establishment of a second front in France go back and read the accounts of the Conn-Louis fight. Let them visualize for a moment the cost, in equipment and life, of an immediate invasion. Let them visualize the waters of the Channel running blood-red under a white moon, and let them visualize the bodies of thousands

124

of British and American soldiers floating in those waters. If the persuasive eloquence of the second-front brigade is followed, no other result is possible. Let them give a second thought to the second front."

That was the picture in June, 1942. There were many things I couldn't say then which I can say now. I couldn't say then that the parachute troops who would be necessary to the establishment of any major offensive were only then being trained. It was not mass production, either. In June, 1942, about 200 parachute troops a week were being graduated from their course. That is all. Nor could I reveal the fact that at that time there were only (comparatively) a handful of American troops finishing their training in Northern Ireland and none at all in Britain. American newspapers carried editorials hinting or sometimes even stating that we had at least a million well-trained, well-equipped men in Ireland and Britain. We would get these papers in London and rush off to Ireland to verify the stories—but, alas, they were only the pipe dreams of the typewriter strategists. Actually at that time we had considerably less than 100,000 men in Ireland.

Our air force hadn't begun to arrive as yet and, had our men been there, there were no airdromes ready for them. That thousand-plane raid on Cologne had strained the facilities of every airdrome in Britain. A few months later enormous, excellent airdromes had been built for the American air force, but you can't build airdromes over night—especially airdromes designed to be used by large bombers which take off loaded to capacity.

These were some of the facts which civilian critics of British and American military leaders did not know. And that is why the Dieppe raid was not the big show, after all—it was merely a dress rehearsal.

7

ROBERTS and Cole and the rest of the staff
thought they'd grab an hour of sleep. I
thought it might be a good idea myself. However, that wasn't as easy as it might have been.
The steward, a little Yorkshireman named Joe
Crowther, went from cabin to cabin, looking for
a bunk, but every one was occupied. Even inside
there were no lights showing. I had a tiny flashlight. I had to keep flashing it, or I would have
stumbled over sleeping forms. It was completely

dark on deck, and even here men were sleeping. Our destroyer, never built to accommodate passengers, was certainly packed tonight. I went back to the wardroom. Ten men lay on the floor, asleep, but there was one vacant chair. It was a straight-backed chair and not very comfortable. On the wall there was a small, swinging set of shelves which held books. Most of them were on navigation, and there was only one that looked interesting. It was called *Dover to Ostend* and under the title in brackets the phrase "A Cross-Channel Thriller." It was by Taffrail. It didn't seem very exciting to such a sucker for detective stories as myself. Fortunately I had a better one in my knapsack and, sitting there in the straight, hard chair, I read that. The hours passed slowly, sitting there with Joe Crowther. It developed that he liked what the British call "thrillers," and we argued amiably as to the relative merits of James Hadley Chase and Peter Cheney, Britain's two most famous exponents of the hard-boiled type of fiction.

Boyle came in, looking incredibly young and eager-eyed.

"Well, we didn't get our heads blown off, after all," I said.

128

"That's right," he said cheerfully. "I never thought we would, you know. You can come on the bridge if you wish."

I did wish. I was surprised to find that we had practically stopped. Evidently we were almost there. Far ahead a light blinked. It seemed strange to see a light showing through the blackness of the night.

"That's a lighthouse," one of the officers on the bridge told me grimly. "It's good news, too. It means they don't expect us. If they did, they'd never keep that blinking. It gives our navigators a chance to check up."

"Where are we now?" I asked.

"About ten miles off Dieppe, directly off the harbor, that is, in the center of the operation," he explained.

Although it was dark ahead, I knew from my session with the maps and from Roberts' explanations just where we were. Directly in front of us was the city of Dieppe. Looking ahead, the city itself was on the right bank of the River Arques. This basin wasn't very wide, but it ran about a mile inland. Obviously, the main force, which had Dieppe itself for its objective, would have to land to the right of the harbor. A shale beach

129

stretched from the harbor to the right for about eight miles. The beach in front of the city itself was a mile long, seventy-five yards in depth, and it had a low sea wall which RAF photos showed to be heavily barbed-wired. The timetable called for three groups of Canadians to land on this beach. The Essex Scottish would land on the part just to the right of the harbor, directly facing the city. About a half mile to the right of them the Royal Hamilton Light Infantry would land, followed by the Calgary Regiment bringing sappers and Churchill tanks with them. They, in turn, were to be followed by the Les Fusiliers Mount Royal. Even before any of them landed, No. 4 Commando was to land some six miles to the right of the harbor on a beach which fronted the district called Varengeville. These experienced Commandos, under brilliant, young Lieutenant Colonel Lord Lovat, had a difficult job to do. They had to knock out the six-inch gun battery at Varengeville. This was an absolute "must," and the night before Lovat had told his men simply, "Our orders are to take a six-inch howitzer battery at Varengeville. We've got to knock it out or the whole operation fails. Do it even at the greatest possible risk."

130

Lovat had led his unit on several raids already. Lovat, a young, good-looking Scottish peer, didn't look the tough type. Before the war, his chief preoccupation had been racing, and no Ascot meeting was complete without the presence of the good-looking, rather vague, young darling of society. Had you told any of his friends, in those days, that underneath that smiling, almost foppish, exterior there hid the soul and iron sinew of the perfect operational military leader, they would have laughed loudly. But Lord Lovat had proven himself in many raids. Lovat is the most ruthless, cold-blooded fighting man I have ever met. To him the war is as simple as this:

"The Germans will not be beaten until most of them are killed. My job is to kill Germans because only by doing that I can help my country win. I do not regard men who have already killed about 50,000 civilians in Britain as anything but beasts, so I do not feel I am committing murder when I kill them."

I doubt if Lovat will live long, but he won't wear out, as do so many of Britain's peers. He'll go out in a blaze of fire and smoke, and his gun or his knife will be the last thing about him that stops flashing. With Lovat in command, you

131

just knew that we wouldn't be bothered much by the six-inch guns from Varengeville.

I stood there on the bridge, gazing at the scene ahead. Dark ships were around us, now moving silently into position. I knew that Lovat's men were disembarking now from their transports; climbing into their landing barges; adding final touches of black to their faces, so that they would blend into the night, fingering their long, black knives and swearing softly to kill the nervousness that even Commandos or American Marines feel at times.

Now let's complete the picture of what the operation to the right of the harbor was to be. Pourville lay about halfway between Dieppe and Varengeville. The South Saskatchewan Regiment was to land there and flank the high ramp which began one mile to the right of Dieppe and stretched the mile and a quarter to Pourville. In back of the ramp and about half a mile to the left of Pourville, the RAF photographs showed that a radio detection finder was located. This was to be destroyed or, if possible, dismantled and brought back by the South Saskatchewan Regiment or by the Queen's Own Cameron Highlanders who were to follow them. A civilian was

132

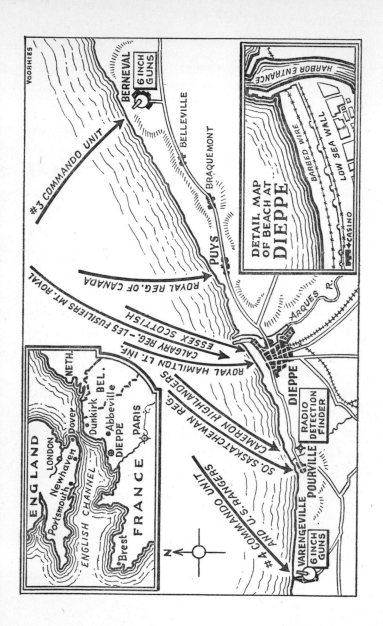

VOORHIES

#3 COMMANDO UNIT

BERNEVAL
6 INCH GUNS

BELLEVILLE

BRAQUEMONT

PUYS

ROYAL REG. OF CANADA

LES FUSILIERS MT. ROYAL

ESSEX SCOTTISH

CALGARY REG. — ROYAL HAMILTON LT. INF.

CAMERON HIGHLANDERS

SO. SASKATCHEWAN REG.

#4 COMMANDO UNIT AND U.S. RANGERS

ARQUES R.

DIEPPE

POURVILLE

RADIO DETECTION FINDER

VARENGEVILLE
6 INCH GUNS

DETAIL MAP OF BEACH AT DIEPPE

HARBOR ENTRANCE

BARBED WIRE

LOW SEA WALL

CASINO

ENGLAND
LONDON
Newhaven
Portsmouth
Dover
ENGLISH CHANNEL
NETH.
Dunkirk
BEL.
Abbeville
DIEPPE
PARIS
FRANCE
Brest

N

to accompany the South Saskatchewan lads—a very important civilian. He was Professor "Wendell" and Professor "Wendell's" real name is known to very few people in Britain. Actually, he is the developer of new stunts in radio location. He is responsible for the immense improvement in this new branch of defensive warfare, and it is due to him that the RAF and anti-aircraft groups in Britain are always able to spot the Germans long before they arrive at their objectives.

I remember, one night when a lot of us were sitting around the Savoy. An alert had been sounded, and it seemed silly to go to bed. After nearly a year's freedom from air raids in London, we didn't quite know how to take them in stride any more. We sat around waiting for what might develop. I was with Larry Rue of the *Chicago Tribune*, Ned Russell of the UP, Red Mueller of *Newsweek*, Erich Baume of an Australian syndicate, Aneurin Bevin, the Labor M.P., and a few others. When raiders are overhead, you argue about silly things. It happened at a time when most of us were broke and someone inevitably asked, "How could any of us make a million dollars quickly?" Each of us had what seemed to be a perfectly reasonable suggestion. Someone pro-

134

posed that a million dollars could be made very quickly if one discovered a cure for cancer; someone else said that anyone who could dream up the knack of reading tomorrow's newspaper today, could make a million dollars very quickly; a third presented the brilliant idea that anyone who could invent a death ray which would destroy enemy planes, tanks and ships could write his own ticket on the British Treasury, and then one, more practical-minded than the rest of us said, "Capture Professor 'Wendell' and get him to Germany. Goering would give a million dollars in cash on the line just to have him, so he could feed him some of that truth serum and learn about the British methods of locating approaching planes and ships."

That won the prize, because we all knew that the Germans would pay anything to have the Professor with them. He would be assured of kindly treatment—oh, such kindly treatment. Nothing would happen to him as long as the whole scientific fund of information lodged in his professorial mind was not exhausted.

Anyhow, this is the civilian who was to accompany the South Saskatchewans on their flank movement. It was not a very pleasant assignment.

135

Professor "Wendell" had a bodyguard of four soldiers whose only job was to stay close to him. From the time they landed on the beach in front of Pourville, they were to ignore the Germans and keep their eyes on the Professor. They were to keep not only their eyes but their drawn guns on the Professor. The Professor was to look over the German radio-detection finder located just behind the wall to find out if there was anything new about it. With his immense technical experience in this sort of thing, a few minutes alone with it should suffice. But suppose the Germans proved to be too strong? Suppose they surprised the Professor and his four bodyguards with the drawn guns? The answer was simple. The four soldiers had orders to shoot the Professor immediately. Britain could not afford to have this genius of radio location fall into enemy hands. The drug which sounds as though it came out of a comic strip was no joke to Mountbatten and his aides. They knew that no man alive had the will power to combat the influence of a drug that has just one property—it makes you tell the truth. Far better to kill "Wendell" than to have him fall into the hands of the Germans, who would make him reveal the secrets that have made

136

the British radio finders the best in the world.
"Wendell" knew the great risk he ran. His sense
of patriotism and his scientific curiosity as to what
the Germans might have in the way of something
new, I am sure, conquered any feeling of fear he
might have entertained.

The Office of Combined Operations will neither
confirm nor deny the presence of Professor
"Wendell" on the raid. However, I know the story
to be true and I know that it was his own idea
that he be killed rather than fall into German
hands. Fortunately for him and for us, he escaped
after accomplishing his task.

That about completes the picture of the beach
to the right of Dieppe—a beach only about eight
miles long. I thought of all this, standing there
on the bridge looking ahead. Now let us consider
for a moment the operation which was (on paper)
to take place to the left of the harbor—and of
Dieppe. Berneval was about seven miles to the
left of the city. There was a six-inch gun battery
here on high ground which commanded both the
harbor and the beaches in front of the city. This,
like the battery at Varengeville, had to be knocked
out and No. 3 Commando was given this task.
Between Berneval and Dieppe was the small vil-

lage of Puys, and the Royal Regiment of Canada (Lieutenant Colonel D. E. Catto commanding) was to land there.

That was the simple outline of the plan. Once both six-inch batteries were knocked out and the landing force had established themselves, a naval unit consisting chiefly of motor-torpedo boats was to slip into the harbor and destroy whatever shipping was there.

And now we were only ten miles from our objective, and the calm darkness ahead, broken only by the blinking of the lighthouse, seemed to indicate that up to now everything was working well. Obviously we hadn't been detected. Closer our flotilla crept, not in single file now but spread out with transports, tank-landing barges and motor-torpedo boats separating and aiming for the particular beach which was their objective. I looked at my watch. It was just 4:10 A. M. And then . . .

The night that had been sleeping awakened brilliantly in a riot of dazzling green and bright-red streaks that arched the sky, flashing vividly against the black velvet of the night. We stood there, stunned, on the bridge. These were tracer bullets, hundreds of them, and they came from

138

our left. What had happened? To the left were the Royals and No. 3 Commando. Were they the targets?

"I'll bet it's that Polish destroyer we brought along," someone growled. "Jumped the gun when they saw something. They were too anxious."

Then again red and green tracer bullets arose lazily into the air, and the sharp bark of ack-ack guns came across the water. It was a beautiful display of fireworks that might have been appreciated another time under different circumstances. They flamed incredible distances across the sky and then melted into the darkness.

"Their radio stuff picked up the sound of our M.T.B. engines," an officer speculated. "They think our aircraft are above. They haven't spotted us."

The ack-ack kept up, but so did the stuff down low, and we knew that they must be aiming at our boats. A speaking tube connected Hughes-Hallett with General Roberts' cabin. They talked. Hughes-Hallett gave orders calmly, unhurriedly. A couple of destroyers, unseen by us, saw the dots and dashes blinked from our bridge. They would go and investigate. This was a disheartening development. There had been no bombing during the night of the stretch between Varenge-ville and Berneval. A real concentrated bombing by three or four hundred bombers an hour before the landing might well have knocked any big guns out and considerably weakened the German defenses, but the element of surprise would then have been completely forfeited. And now some unknown element had entered the picture; that unforeseen, incalculable accident had happened, and we did not have the advantage which the bombing would have given us. They knew now that we were here.

The answer to the firing came soon. Boyle returned from General Roberts' cabin.

"A tanker was going in, a few miles to the left of Dieppe. It was escorted by four or five E boats. They saw our Commandos and started giving them hell. Now we've got some destroyers over there, but," he added gloomily, "this will upset our schedule."

"It'll upset the whole dam works, won't it?"

Boyle shook his head. "Of course not! We go ahead as planned. They don't know what's up. It'll delay the No. 3 Commando group though, and the Royals. They can't get through that barrage until the E boats are finished. The Royals

140

were scheduled to land at 4:50. It's almost that now and they can't get close. This means they'll have to land in the dawn."

"That's bad."

He nodded grimly. "That'll be bad."

I went back to the bridge and through my mind the old rhyme went—"For want of a nail the shoe was lost, for want of a shoe . . ." It would be tragic if this chance encounter with a tanker ruined the whole show. And yet the fact that the tanker was approaching the harbor gave added evidence that our visit was an unexpected one. We had two bits of evidence as to that now: the lighthouse flashing and the tanker's presence. Our destroyer moved in closer, and now a faint dilution of the night to the east told us that the dawn would soon be here. The approach of dawn was never hailed with less enthusiasm than this one. If it could hold off long enough so the Commandos could land in darkness and silence that six-inch gun battery at Berneval, things might still work out. Happily there was no sound, and there were no red and green streaks piercing the darkness of the right flank—Lovat's men were apparently working unmolested. I looked at the

141

timetable. They would be landing now, and with them were a few American Rangers.

"Murder 'em, kids," I breathed, half aloud, and then realized that I was in the position of my favorite comic-strip character, Wimpey, who, when attacked, always hid behind his friend Popeye and said, "Let's you and him fight." We on the bridge of the destroyer were so far quite removed from it all—the tracers were at least four miles to our left. I went into Roberts' cabin and sat on the floor close to the door, out of the way. Roberts and Cole talked calmly, and three men with earphones and mouthpieces received reports and then gave them to Roberts.

"The E boats have been dispersed. Three of them sunk. The tanker has been destroyed. No. 3 Commando and the Royal Regiment are trying to find their rendezvous and proceed." This was a typical report.

It was an hour later before we heard the full report. The fire from the E boats had scattered the landing barges filled with Commandos. E boats are overgrown motor-torpedo boats. They are about 117 feet long and, in addition to torpedoes, they carry fifty-caliber machine guns and anti-aircraft guns. They are fast as the devil

142

and twice as nasty. The landing barges had to scatter. Some of them were hit and sunk. Many, many of the Commandos died before ever reaching shore. The others turned back. But one landing barge managed to flank the E boats unobserved. It crept toward shore and finally "touched down" (to use the Commando's term) on the beach. In this barge were a group of men not actually combat Commandos. They had been trained as liaison and communication orders. But they carried guns. They waited for a few moments on the beach and then Major Peter Young, M. C., the only officer with them, said, "We got orders to put that six-inch battery out of action, didn't we?"

Someone said, "That's right."

"Then what the hell are we waiting for?" twenty-four-year-old Peter Young said, and out they piled. They found a series of steps cut in the high wall. They felt that it might be mined, but now daylight was ready to break and they couldn't waste precious minutes investigating. They cut the barbed wire and climbed the steps. There were only twenty men. They went inland a quarter of a mile, still unobserved, and then they saw the six-inch battery. They scattered, Indian fashion, and opened fire

143

with their little Sten guns. Their fire was accurate. It harried the Germans manning the guns. These twenty crawled from tree to tree and the Germans thought they were five hundred. They couldn't silence the battery, but they worried it so by their sniping that we, lying off shore, never got its full attention. They gave Peter Young the D.S.O. for that.

I went on deck and now the dawn was growing brighter. It looked frail and a bit delicate—incongruous visitor to this part of the world dedicated today to murder. I looked at my watch and at our timetable. Now our naval guns were all to blast away at the beaches in front of Dieppe and further to the right. The beach measured 1,780 yards, and our destroyers were to send 1,780 shells screaming at it. Each destroyer had a sector to cover. The barrage opened as the second hand of my watch hit the minute. All watches had been synchronized the night before. The barrage began and the air seemed to tremble and vibrate with the sound. The guns thundered and golden flashes cut the half light of the dawn. For ten minutes this Wagnerian overture continued and then, as though it had all been rehearsed by a master director, the curtain of the night rolled up,

144

the sun chased a few wisps of mist away, and in front of us lay the city of Dieppe. At first the white smoke from the shell explosions hid the cliffs to the right, but a breeze hurried from across the Channel to waft the smoke away and now the whole operational field lay before us. Several lazy spirals of black smoke arose from the city, and I remembered that Douglas Bostons were to bomb Dieppe during that ten minutes of naval shelling. They had done their job, had climbed into the upper story of the sky, and were hurrying home for breakfast. We hadn't as yet heard or seen one hostile aircraft and we had been here for nearly an hour and a half. Why hadn't the Luftwaffe come after us? We were sitting birds there outside the harbor of Dieppe. Then I realized that this was one more piece of evidence to prove that our visit had been a complete surprise to them. Had they expected us, bomber aircraft would have been waiting at near-by Abbeville, at a dozen other airdromes east and west of Dieppe. They would have been here long ago blasting us with their bombs. But they weren't here and that was a good omen.

From the left flank came dull booms from the six-inch guns and we knew that No. 3 Commando hadn't been able to do its job as yet. We didn't know about those heroic twenty as yet. Then came the once-heard-never-forgotten rattle of machine-gun fire. But cutting through it all and above the guns and the sound of a hundred engines came a high singing and even I knew that was the sound of the Spitfires. I looked back and saw black dots that grew and grew, and the joyous chorus of their engines swelled and then they were above us, circling sedately, and then coming lower in feigned curiosity as though to ask, "My, my, what's going on here?" There were twenty-four of them—two squadrons, and they looked very beautiful. Spitfires are very beautiful. There is a dainty slimness about them that no other planes have. Their motors never roar—they hum and sing. Now they broke formation, swinging into flights of four each. They separated and hit different levels so that we would be protected from all sides. Each flight had a Tail-End Charlie whose job was to weave right, left, up, down, so that no Jerry plane could surprise his group of four planes. The others circled steadily, making believe not to notice the childish antics of Tail-End Charlie as he slipped and banked and turned in aimless-looking but meticulously arranged pat-

146

terns. I looked at my timetable to see what squadrons these might be. I caught my breath when I saw Squadrons 72 and 121. They were due at this time—my Eagle Squadron guys. I looked up and felt warm at heart. I knew every one of those pilots up there. I'd lived with them at their airports and they'd lived with me when they hit London.

It is hard for one squadron to stand out in the RAF. The whole RAF is damned good, but Squadron 72 always did stand out. This was the first Eagle Squadron, and I'd known them from the beginning. There were only a very few of the original pilots left. I looked up and wondered which was Pete's Spitfire. That was Squadron Leader Chesley Gordon Peterson, D.F.C., of Provo, Utah, a dyed-in-the-wool Mormon. Pete had been married a week or so before to a lovely English girl. Pete was up there all right, and that grinning little devil, Gussie, beside him. That was Squadron Leader Guy Daymond, D.F.C. He'd been working around Hollywood two years before, and now he was one of the greatest shots in the RAF. I remember Pete once saying, "Any time Gussie gets a Jerry in his sights, that Jerry is one dead pigeon." I thought of big Flight Lieutenant

Oscar Coen who went from the University of Wisconsin to join the Eagles. Old Oscar was up there, all right. There were some who wouldn't be there. Bill Geiger wouldn't, and Red Tobin and Jack Fessler and Andy Mamedoff and Bill Hall and Danny Daniels. The war was over for them.

I knew Squadron 121 just as well. I'd been at their mess only two weeks before, and it had been fun because there was a pool in a small city near-by and the pilots were allowed the free use of it. They had a good cook, too, and a grand squadron leader; he was English and his name was Hugh Kennard. He was up there now with his 121 bunch. Good-looking Jimmy Daley, D.F.C., was up there, probably whistling "Deep in the Heart of Texas." He'd been in my place a few days before and had turned on the radio. A band was playing his favorite song.

"You see," he drawled, "even here in London they got to sing about my state."

Jimmy Du Four from Oakland would be there. He'd just been married. One morning a letter came to me from New York. It was a short note and it read, "Take a couple of RAF pilots out and give them a good time." It was signed by Joe, Harry, Frank and Hal Stevens. They are the big-

148

gest outdoor caterers in the world, and they are known in baseball and racing circles to own the four biggest hearts in the world. From the envelope there fluttered a check for $150. So with that Flight Lieutenant Jimmy Du Four and his bride had a great wedding party. The boys had all come to London for it. We'd turned the old Savoy lopsided that night. Pilot Officer Barry Mahon, a smiling kid and a great one for going on rhubarbs on his own, was there that night and he was up there now. I hadn't heard from Barry for three or four weeks, so one day I phoned him at the mess, just to be sure he was all right.

"All right?" he had laughed. "Sure, I'm all right. Don't you know nothin' ever happens to *you*? It always happens to the other guy."*

Yes, it was thrilling to look up at those slim Spitfires and feel that I knew every one of the pilots up there by his first name—that I was accepted by them as one of them, even though I didn't know one end of an airplane from another. Too bad, I thought, that Jack Mooney had to miss this show. He would have loved it. Flight Lieutenant Mooney of Long Island City was a

*Since the Dieppe raid Pilot Officer Mahon has been taken a prisoner of war.

tall, handsome youngster. He and Jimmy Du Four
of Oakland were the two Flight Lieutenants of
Squadron 121. Squadron Leader Hugh Kennard,
of course, led the group, but when a squadron
attacks it usually attacks in flights of four planes
and Du Four and Mooney each led a flight.
Mooney was going to be married last July fourth.
I remember getting an invitation to his wedding.
I'd answered it and said I'd love to be there and
had left the invitation on my desk. One afternoon
just before the wedding was to take place Jimmy
Du Four came into my place. He looked down at
my desk and picked up the wedding invitation.

"The wedding is off," he had said casually—
too casually.

"What's the matter?" I asked sharply.

"Jimmy bought it yesterday on a sweep." The
RAF pilots never use the word "killed." They say
of a fellow pilot "He bought it." Looking again
at the circling Spitfires I wondered how many of
them would "buy it" here today.

150

8

ROBERTS kept getting reports—none of them good. Each beach, each objective had been given a name. The beach in front of the city itself was Red Beach—the one in front of Varengeville, Orange Beach.

"Report from Orange Beach, sir," the aide looked up at Roberts. "No. 4 Commando accomplished their mission—returning."

Roberts smiled. "You can depend on them to do their job. What about Red Beach?"

151

The aide shook his head and repeated monoton-
ously, "Calling Red Beach. Calling Red Beach."
This was where No. 3 Commando was to land.

"Blue Beach?" Roberts was thoughtful. There
was no report from Blue Beach. This was the
beach in front of Puys which the Royals had for
their objective. No report, and Roberts shifted
uneasily in his chair. This was an intensely personal matter with him. He had helped plan the
attack; had backed General McNaughton's insistence that this be a Canadian show. He had trained
this Canadian Army, knew every officer in it. To
me the Royal Regiment of Canada was a military
unit. To Roberts it was Colonel Catto and Joe
Smith and Harry Bledsoe and a lot of men he
knew. But this was no time for him to think too
much of men. He had to think of regiments as
machines. He had to think of men as cogs in the
machine. The Germans had made the rules in this
game, and if you played any other rules they'd
knock you silly.

But it was hard to sit there visualizing what
was happening only five miles away. The Royals,
delayed fifteen minutes by the E boat encounter,
had been forced to land in daylight. The head-
land behind the beach was undoubtedly bristling

152

with guns and behind that there were four-inch mortars which, from long practice, could drop their shells right on the beach—and among the Royals. It was not a pretty picture.

"Red Beach calling. Asks for more smoke on west (right) cliffs. Being straffed badly."

"Henderson, tell Alfred," Roberts said.

Colonel Henderson, one of Roberts' aides, called into his microphone, "Calling Alfred. Calling Alfred. Lay smoke on west cliffs immediately. Lay smoke on west cliffs immediately. Are you getting me? Over."

"Alfred" today was RAF headquarters in England. Somewhere three hundred miles away ears glued to headsets heard that. Orders were given. We had Douglas Bostons hovering over us, equipped with two-way wireless. I walked on deck and looked toward the white cliffs to the right. They rose cleanly from the beach fringed at the top with green. Two Bostons, unmistakable with their two motors, their long glass nose, and their general air of trimness, seemed to dive from nowhere. They trailed white feathery smoke behind them and it settled on the cliffs. They were flying, it seemed, less than fifty feet above the top of the cliffs. There was so much noise now that it had all merged, and I couldn't distinguish the bark of the ack-ack guns and the machine guns I knew were shooting at the Bostons. They banked sharply just before reaching the city of Dieppe and turned to retrace their flight. Again white smoke trailed from them and now the tops of the cliffs were hidden by this artificial layer of cloud. Machine gunners there would not be able to see our men huddling behind the low seawall on the beach.

This was the essence of Combined Operations. Not two minutes had passed since General Roberts had asked for smoke on the cliffs—and now the cliffs were shrouded with it. This was the Mountbatten way—swift, sure, calculated. Land, air, naval forces were all acting as a team. There was no conflict of authority, no personalities entered into the team work of this group. It was like a very great football team which is so good that no one star can be singled out.

We had moved closer inshore now, and the scene was something that Hollywood could not have duplicated. It was unbelievable, and you had to shake your head to realize that this was all real. Shells still came from the batteries at Varengeville. One landed fifty feet from us and

154

threw up a huge cascade of water which, catching
the rays of the sun, fell back throwing off red
and golden sparks. Boats of every kind were
around us, stretching as far as the eye could see.
Small motor launches dashed from ship to ship.
Motor-torpedo boats roared throatily by, and large
barges filled to the gunwales with men and guns
were moving in towards the shore—these were
the reserves or follow-up troops. Tank-landing
barges lumbered up. Two of our ships (both
small) burned lazily and casually, and the smoke
from them almost hung in the sky, for now there
was no breeze.

A landing craft approached us, tied up and men
climbed on board. They were dirty and grimy
and their faces were streaked with black, but
they were grinning. This was part of Lovat's No.
4 bunch. They hadn't been able to locate their
own ship so they'd come to us.

"How was it?" I asked a big Commando as he
climbed on deck.

"A piece of cake," he laughed. The Commandos
evidently had borrowed the RAF slang. In the
RAF a "piece of cake" means "it was a cinch,
nothing to it."

"Did you get that six-inch battery?"

155

He roared. "Hey," he called to men who were climbing on board, "this bloke asks did we get that six-inch battery."

They all laughed, and then the big Commando stiffened and said, "Sorry, sir," as he saw the two silver colonel's leaves on my shoulder. I'd forgotten about them.

"I'm a phony colonel, chum," I told him. "Just for today. I'm a reporter. Tell me about it."

"We 'touched down' on schedule," he said. "There was a wall with barbed wire, but we got over it. We got close to them before they even knew we were there. Then we gave it to them. Oh, we didn't half give it to them. Luck? We were shot with luck. A shell from our mortar hit their magazine and blew the whole bloody works up. So we rushed in and finished them off. They put up a fight, but they don't like that steel. Do they?"

His pals who had gathered around him nodded. "It was very nice," one of them grinned.

"We knocked off their guns and took a few prisoners. We only had room in the boat for a few."

"What did you do with them?"

"Why," he said happily, "we give 'em each a ticket to the Marble Arch Cinema and told them to go to Claridges. We had rooms reserved for them there."

"Do you tie prisoners up when you bring 'em back?"

"No bloody fear," he spat over the rail. "What for? They were too scared to run away. Hell, we were hoping they would. Then we could of give it to them. They're in one of the other barges."

"Tell him about the Colonel," one of the others interrupted.

My big guy roared with laughter. "He's a one —the Colonel. That's Colonel Lovat. Coming back he was last off the beach. He always is—the Colonel. Right?"

"Right," one of them said proudly, "and the first to land."

"Well," he went on, "we were all in the barges. They were about fifteen feet off shore, so they wouldn't get stuck in case of a quick getaway. We all waded out and climbed in, and there was the Colonel on the beach being sure everyone was aboard. They were giving us plenty of hell, too. Those mortars from way back somewhere were dropping close and machine guns from the cliffs were going very fast. Stuff was dropping all over and then, to make it worse, a Focke-Wulf

157

dove at us and give us plenty. The Colonel starts walking out in the water and when it gets to his knees, he's still ten feet from our barge and he lets out a yell, "Why the bloody hell should I get soaking wet because you blokes are too damned lazy to bring the barge in close to shore? Come and get me."

They all roared with laughter. "Stuff falling all around and him only worrying about getting wet," one of them chuckled.

"He sounds like a hell of a man."

"He is a hell of a man."

"There's rum and brandy down in the wardroom. What are you waiting for?" I reminded them. They disappeared, still chuckling.

Above, our Spitfires circled. They could only stay half an hour and then they'd be relieved by other squadrons. A Spitfire has fuel for only an hour and a half. The trip from their airdromes took half an hour, the trip back half an hour, so they could only stay with us half an hour. They were quite low—about 3,000 feet. Their ceiling for the operation had been pegged at 7,000 feet. Today they were not offensive fighters. They were here to protect us. If German bombers wanted to bomb from fifteen thousand feet, let them.

158

With a pall of smoke, which half hid us and then
arose, their bombing from any real height would
be entirely hit or miss. They'd have to come down
low, have to dive, probably. I stood with the
crew of our big ack-ack guns on the main deck.
They had two four-inch guns that shot simultane-
ously. A four-inch fires a very heavy shell; thirty-
five pounds of steel and high explosive.

And then the Luftwaffe came. One of the gun
crew let out a yell, "Over Dieppe," and there, at
5,000 feet, were three Dorniers coming at us, in
formation. Two flights of Spitfires veered quickly.
One flight from the right cut across the cliffs to
get behind the bombers. One Dornier broke formation shooting off to the left. Three Spits chased
it, and then for perhaps five seconds a thin golden
shaft appeared at the nose of each Spitfire. Our
own guns were firing just ahead of the Dornier,
and it seemed to run into the ugly black bursts
from our shells. The Spits got closer and again
the nose and the wings of the leading Spit glowed
with brightness that might have been, but wasn't,
a reflection of the sun. Actually, when a Spit fires,
a two-foot shaft of flame shoots out of its guns
and cannon—at 3,000 feet this looks like a shaft
of light. The one Spit executed a maneuver I'd

never seen before. He dove under the tail of the Dornier and then climbed up under it, firing as he came up, firing into the fat belly of the Dornier and a thin, white trail of smoke appeared, as though the belly were leaking and the white smoke changed to black and the Dornier began a slow dive. Then a burst of bright orange flame completely obliterated the smoke, as though the belly of the Dornier had exploded. The flame blew not backward, oddly enough, but forward, and now the whole nose of the Dornier was a ball of fire as its dive became deeper. A dozen small black specks dropped from the Dornier and they fell fast, traveling at first in the direction the plane was going, as bombs do, and then they fell into the water three hundred yards away. The ship rocked, because water is a great conductor of sound or vibration, and the bombs threw up jets of water. Two more small black specks dropped from the diving plane and then billowed out. Two of the crew had bailed out.

"There's five in a Dornier," one of the sailors yelled, "they got the other three."

The Dornier dove sedately, unhurriedly, with the three Spits following it, as though to make sure it hit the water. It hit with a mighty splash

160

a quarter of a mile from us, and then I looked for the other two.

Three Spits were on the tail of one of them. All seemed to hit it at once. This Dornier died in an orange ball of fire. Evidently its petrol tank had exploded. It was a lovely sight if you hate Germans, and I hate Germans. It settled slowly, with three Spitfires circling it as celestial pallbearers. Then the whole mass plunged into the sea and we ducked behind gun shields and into gangways as bits and pieces of it landed on our decks.

All of our guns were firing now. Our gun crew was potting away at the third Dornier, which had crossed over us and was now veering back toward the shore. Spits were following it. All during this, twelve additional Spitfires kept circling above, paying no attention to the Dorniers at all. Wise in the ways of Luftwaffe fighting, they wouldn't all allow themselves to be drawn into a fight with three enemy airplanes. They knew that more Dorniers and the dreaded Focke-Wulf 190's would follow, and they remembered that their job was to protect—not to follow what might be false trails.

Our guns made a terrific noise and then there

was the shrill swish as the shells left and started upward toward their rendezvous. The gun crew worked in beautiful harmony. Range finders bent over their instruments, men passed shells, men slapped them into guns, breeches slammed shut smoothly. Black bursts seemed to surround the Dornier, and then suddenly there was no Dornier. A shell had hit it squarely. It didn't die spectacularly. It merely came apart. One moment it was streaking at 280 miles an hour, alive, pulsating, vital, and then it was a mass of scattering debris. One wing sluiced crazily down, and thousands of parts too small to see flew in a thousand directions. It was very impersonal, and the thought that men of flesh and blood were parts of that flying debris never presented itself. Aerial warfare is impersonal. I never met a pilot who ever gave a thought to the enemy pilots he had killed. A fighter pilot's job is to down enemy planes; he never thinks of men who are in those planes.

I remembered discussing that once with Wing Commander Malan, D.S.O., D.F.C., probably the greatest of them all. During the battle of Britain, "Sailor" Malan, as he is known to all of Britain, knocked down something like thirty-five German aircraft. Later he had increased the number of his victims when night fighting. He was at my place once and I was finishing a story. He and I were going out somewhere when I finished.

"There's a swell detective story there, Sailor," I told him. "Why don't you start it while I knock off this piece?"

"A book?" Sailor said in surprise. "Hell, I never read a book in my life."

This amazed me because the Sailor was an extremely intelligent and well-informed man.

"Just got no imagination, I guess," he said laconically. "Thank God I haven't. I'd have been dead long ago if I had."

It was then that we got to discussing a pilot's reaction after he has made his kill. We figured up how many enemy planes the Sailor had knocked down in the past two years. Many were bombers carrying a crew of five or six. As close as I could figure he had killed perhaps 250 men. The Sailor looked incredulous.

"I never thought of it that way," he said thoughtfully. "When I'm fighting, I'm fighting enemy aircraft—not men. No, I guess I've got no imagination."

Now, watching that Dornier die and the men with her, I knew what the Sailor meant. Except when you come to close quarters, war is an impersonal thing. Until now (except when you thought of the Royals) this operation was quite impersonal, because we had no wounded aboard to bring home to us what was happening ashore.

Now the Spitfires were buzzing around triumphantly. Three out of three was a pretty good score so far, although the Spits were probably angry that our ack-ack cheated them out of a sure victim. But the assault by the Dorniers was only the beginning. From now on we were under constant pressure from enemy aircraft. Far to the left above land, I could see Spitfires and Focke-Wulfs fighting, tiny specks against the sky. Sometimes you couldn't see the planes, you'd only see feathery white streaks trailing as they dove to attack or escape. Wherever you looked you saw dogfights as Focke-Wulfs and Dorniers tried to break through our protecting umbrellas. I hadn't seen any real air fighting since the days when we sat on the cliffs at Dover, watching the Battle of Britain. So far we had all the best of this fighting, and no bombs had fallen close enough to hurt us.

A landing barge pulled alongside and delivered the first wounded. There were ten of them—all but two walking cases. They lifted two stretchers

164

aboard and I followed them below to where the doctor was waiting. He had a small room two decks below. He told the walking cases to sit down in the passageway while he took care of the two badly wounded. Both men lay there with eyes wide open, saying nothing. Their faces were curiously alike, drained of blood, expressionless, almost as though their pain had fashioned masks for them. The doctor's name was Martin. He pulled the covering back from one stretcher. This man had been shot in the stomach. The doctor's expression didn't change. He took a needle and stuck it into the man's arm. He stood up, looked at me and shrugged his shoulders.

The second man had a leg wound. They lifted him on the table, and the doctor gave him an injection of something. Whatever it was, it seemed to give the man some relief, because his breathing became less labored. The doctor had two orderlies working with him. They hurriedly cut the man's trouser leg and bared the wound completely. I looked, fascinated at first, then horrified. Below his knee the man's leg held only by a shred. It was not a pretty sight, and I turned away.

"How did I get out? How did I get out?" the

voice that came from the man was a dead mono-tone. "We touched down and rolled our tanks out . . . . They hit our first two tanks . . . . We rolled out two more—they hit them . . . . We all stepped ashore and machine guns came from both sides . . . Mortars came from behind the wall . . . . Everyone was hit—except me. I climbed back into the barge . . . . They kept shooting at us . . . . They didn't hit me . . . . The barge drifted and drifted, and another boat came and I got on that boat . . . . They were all killed—all, except me . . . They never hit me . . . .

The voice trailed off into nothingness, but there was no change in expression. The doctor, his lips tight, swore under his breath, "Too late, damn it! Well, get him out, and let's see those men out-side. Bring in the worst ones first."

Only then did I realize that the man on the table was dead. I walked out of the room, feeling a little sick. Our Oerlikon guns were barking angrily, which meant that the enemy planes were still coming. The wardroom was crowded now. At least a dozen men in soaking uniforms were there, and Mess Steward Joe Crowther was help-ing them remove their wet clothes. Some of these

166

men were Commandos with the No. 3 Unit. Others were of the Royal Regiment. They all looked completely exhausted. Several of them had clumsy bandages on their arms and legs.

"Doctor will be here soon," little Crowther soothed. "Meanwhile, what about a drink? A brandy will warm you up, and it's all on the house."

They swallowed large gulps of the brandy and choked and nobody said much. They'd been through a bad time and, to make it worse, they knew that they hadn't accomplished their objective. Oh, it wasn't their fault, but the frustrated feeling of failure hung heavily on them.

"They threw everything at us," one of them told me. "We had to land in daylight. There was a wall and they had machine guns on top of it. We had to get close. We ran to the wall and hugged it and they couldn't get us then. But we couldn't do much, either."

I walked up the iron ladders to Roberts' office. He was as calm and unruffled as ever. He smoked one cigarette after another and kept a large cup of hot tea beside him. I sat on the floor listening to the reports.

167

"Guess we won't get ashore," he said to me, "too much to do here."

That was a tough decision for Roberts to make. Roberts is quite definitely what men call a "fighting general." Had things gone according to plan, he would have landed in front of the Casino and directed the occupation of Dieppe from there. But now his men to the left on the beaches in front of Puys were in grave danger. He would be of no help to them, standing on the beach by the Casino, five miles away. Only here, where he had the ears of the whole operation, where he could be the eyes of the whole operation and its guiding force, could he be of help.

"Red Beach calling," the voice came, calmly, through the loud speaker. "We are being strafed by Focke-Wulfs. Situation serious."

"Get Spitfires over there immediately. Tell Red Beach they're coming," Roberts said.

His Royals were at Red Beach. This was that nasty spot in front of Puys where they had been forced to land by daylight. Orders were spoken into microphones. It was comforting to know that within two minutes Spits would be over there dealing with the Focke-Wulf. Down low a Spitfire is a match for a Focke-Wulf 190. Up high,

168

nothing can touch it—nothing, but the Spitfire 9, and only a certain number of those were in combat. It was hard not to think of those men crouching in the dubious shelter of low walls, behind rocks, hearing the scream of Focke-Wulfs and then the tearing of their cannon and machine guns. They had only their rifles and their sten guns, futile toys against a plane going 350 miles an hour; a plane heard but hardly seen.

I went back to the wardroom.

9

THERE were about fifteen men in the ward-room now, half of them lying on the floor. Joe Crowther had helped them off with their clothes and had wrapped them in heavy blankets. The doctor went from one to another. Most of the wounds were shrapnel wounds, and those aren't so bad unless you are hit in the stomach. The shrapnel was mostly in small bits, but Martin didn't have time to dig the bits out. He had time only to pour disinfectant over the wounds and slap a bandage pad over them.

170

"Best I can do is give first aid," he said. "No time for surgery, except for a few critical cases. Maybe you can help. Joe, give me a bottle of brandy."

He handed me a bottle of brandy and an armful of bandages. The bandages were thick pads about four inches square, and they had court-plaster stickers at each corner, so that part of it was easy. One man the doctor hadn't reached lay there with a bleeding arm. I bent over him and poured the brandy on the wound.

"That smarts like hell," he grumbled. Then the doctor yelled at me, "No, no. Here's some Mercurochrome for that. Don't pour the brandy over the wounds. Give them a drink of brandy; they're chilled; it'll warm them up."

They all laughed and started to kid me, and that was all right.

"You must be a teetotaler," one of them said, "throwing away good brandy like that."

"God forbid," I shuddered. The doctor hurried aft to his little dressing room where the ugly cases awaited him. Occasionally a bomb fell fairly close, and down below the water line we were never sure whether we had received a direct hit or not. We'd hear an explosion and the ship would creak

171

and list a bit, and we'd be quiet and then Joe
Crowther would laugh and say, "Hell, that was
half a mile away." Joe Crowther had been merely
a Yorkshire accent a few hours before. Now he
was emerging as a personality. He had a moon
face and large pale eyes and he talked very
slowly.

"This is a lucky ship," he said, wrapping a new-
comer in blankets. "They may get every other ship
in the show but not this one. Aye, she's been
through a lot; been hit lots of times, but they
can't hurt her. She's sturdy and honest, she is, and
best of all she's lucky. Have a drop of brandy,
mate. It's all on His Majesty, the King. There'll
be no mess bills this day."

Someone stumbled down the iron ladder just
outside the door leading into the wardroom and
a form lurched in. He looked familiar and then
I saw that it was Wallace Reyburn of the *Montreal
Standard*. His face was ashen. He took two steps
into the room and then collapsed slowly to the
floor. He lay there, completely out. Joe Crowther
unbuttoned his wet tunic. Somehow you automatically start looking to see if a man has a
belly wound. If he has, you yell for the doctor.
If he hasn't, why, then, you feel that he's all

172

right. Joe tore the clothes away from his stomach, but there was no blood. I leaned over Wally and lifted his head and forced some brandy down his throat. He choked and shook his head, opened his eyes and recognized me.

"This is a hell of a story, isn't it?" he grinned weakly, and then passed out.

He was lying there after emerging from a nightmare; he was wounded somewhere, and his face was white and the skin was drawn tightly over the cheekbones; for all he knew he might be dying, and yet his first conscious thought was, "This is a hell of a story." Neither the *Montreal Standard* nor any paper in the world could buy loyalty like that; no school of journalism in the world could train a man to that. I felt humble in the presence of this (to me) youngster. This was a newspaperman. I felt very proud of my profession then. I hardly knew Wally. He had only been in London a few months—just one of many youngsters who had come over recently. But I knew him now; I'd always know him, and respect him, and remember that line, "This is a hell of a story, isn't it?"

Then he came to and this time the brandy stayed down. He was only exhausted, I thought.

173

He stood up and we helped him get his clothes off.

"I'm not sure, but I think I got hit a couple of times," he said. Joe and I investigated. He had been hit in the shoulder and someplace else.

"There's one wound you'll never be able to show anyone," I laughed. "You'll never be able to see it yourself unless you're a contortionist. It isn't bad—just a little shrapnel. I can pluck it out—some of it. It's out. There's more under the skin. Does it hurt?"

He shook his head. Not one of the men complained of pain during those long hours. The shock of the whole experience apparently acted as an anesthetic. Nerves were perhaps too numb to deliver messages of pain. Joe wrapped Wally in blankets and put him in a chair. Joe had rubbed him dry and he was comfortable enough.

"How was it on shore?" I asked.

"Bloody awful," he shivered. "It was with the Saskatchewans. We landed on the beach at Pourville and you should have heard our heavy boots on the pebbles of that beach—loudest sound I ever heard—but they never got wise. There was a twelve-foot parapet there and we had to get over it. On top was barbed wire and very tough

174

barbed wire. Our guys worked and worked and finally one of them cut through it and we went over there. That's when they discovered us. There was an empty blockhouse just behind, and we ducked into that. It looked like it hadn't been used for a long time. The machine-gun bullets spattered outside, but this was a good blockhouse. It was fine until I suddenly got the thought that it might be mined, and that this was just a trap. Well, I was right—but it wasn't a trap for us. Anyhow, they weren't ready to spring it. An hour later the Camerons followed us, and when they were in the blockhouse they sprung it and killed a lot of them."

"You left the blockhouse?"

"Then we went to a deserted house. But they started tossing mortars at us and that wasn't good. So we established headquarters in a grassy strip a little way from the house. They had the house taped, you see, and could drop mortars right on it. The boys brought in some prisoners. Our officers questioned them, and then a shell landed right in the midst of us all. I was lying down, and it felt like pebbles were dropping on my back. That's when I got hit, though I didn't know it. That concussion was making my ears ring so I

175

couldn't feel anything. Four German prisoners
were killed by the shell. Then they started throwing everything at us."

"It must have been tough."

"That was an alarm clock, I guess, though I
couldn't figure it out at the time." He was very
thoughtful.

"Better have another drink of brandy," I said,
thinking he was going back to that nether-nether
world.

"We were passing a farmhouse and all of a
sudden a bell started going off—a shrill bell. I
wondered what the hell it was. It must have been
an alarm clock. Well, that farmer didn't need an
alarm clock to wake him this morning. Anyhow,
we started to go to the city itself. We had to cross
a river and there was a bridge across it. The
first men who went over were all mowed down.
Our stretcher bearers dashed in and brought
some of them back. Then Merritt came up. That's
Colonel C. C. I. Merritt, and what a man! A big,
young-looking guy, only thirty-three. A terrific
guy. He just turned to his men and said calmly,
"Don't bunch up. Here we go." And then, carrying his tin hat in his hand, he just walked across
that bridge like he was taking a stroll. Every-

176

thing was flying at him but he just strolled along. That's guts. Last I saw of him, he was going on toward Dieppe with a gun in each hand. I hope he gets back."

He had to stop. Both our Oerlikons and our four-inch guns were firing, and the noise and vibration of them filled the small room. The lamp over the table began swinging from side to side crazily. We listed badly to port and then to starboard—we were zigzagging, zigzagging. Evidently the Jerry planes were getting through. The bombs were hitting closer, too. Additional wounded had come in. They lay there quietly, not saying a word, but somehow you could hear their unuttered cries of shock and pain—and they too filled the room, mingling with the noise and the vibration and the horrible smell of cordite and gun powder that seeped in. Every time our four-inch guns went, the whole ship trembled. Then several things happened at once.

I guess the lurch came first, a split second before the explosion. The ship heaved upward and then lurched to port. And then the explosion came, and it kept ringing in your ears for minutes. It was as though you'd hit a giant glass with a giant tuning fork, and the sound of it kept on long

177

after the blow had been struck. This was a tearing, searing explosion, and then from the pantry adjoining the wardroom there was a mighty rush of water. We all hung onto tables and chairs, and still the wounded who lay there never moved or moaned. This all in the space of four seconds, and then above it all came a ringing laugh. Not a hysterical laugh, but a healthy, hearty, belly laugh. It had come from Joe Crowther.

"Hear that gun of ours?" his Yorkshire voice boomed. That's our new eight-inch gun. Sounds just like a bomb hittin' us, don't it? Hell of a gun, that big eight-inch. We're a little small for such a big gun. Shakes the ship up a bit. Even loosened a plate or two in the pantry and broke all my glasses."

I looked at Joe's big innocent moonlike face and I blessed him. We had no eight-inch guns on our ship. Some of the tenseness which had gripped the wounded men left them a little bit. We were far below the water line and there would be small chance of getting up the iron ladder if we started to sink. Every gangway, every passageway was choked now with the wounded. Some life came back to the faces of the men who lay in the wardroom.

178

"That deserves a drink all around," Joe Crowther called out cheerily. Some of these men were officers. However, Joe Crowther, steward, was definitely the boss here. "No more glasses," he said cheerfully. "Got to drink from the bottle. Take a good one, it's all on the house. It's all on the King today."

Men were hurrying into the pantry with tools. The ship had righted itself, but now we were zigzagging again. The planes hadn't been driven off.

"We're laying a smoke screen," Crowther said calmly. "We always zigzag when we do that."

Then for a while—a very little while—it was calm enough. We hardly heard the Oerlikons or the fifty calibers or the four-inch guns now after that earlier cataclysm. It may have been that we were all a little stunned. I wondered idly how many men had been killed up there on deck, on the open bridge.

"How long were you on shore, Wally?" I asked.

"Six and a half hours," he said. "Bloody long hours. The last hour was the worst. Our boats were due at eleven o'clock to take us off. That last hour we just waited. Then they came—right on the dot. The tide was out, and we had to run three hundred yards to reach them. That was a

179

long three hundred yards because we were getting machine-gunned from both ends of the beach and from the rear high explosives stuff and mortar shells were being tossed at us. I got out to a boat, and the damned thing was stuck. Then there was a roar and a Focke-Wulf dove at us, giving us plenty of cannon and machine gun. We pushed the boat out and then damned if a wave didn't push it back again. I looked around the beach. It was like Dunkirk must have been; men lying there, wounded or dead; men up to their knees in water, waiting for boats; men aiming their sten guns and rifles at planes that passed so fast you could hardly see them. We got the boat off and were out fifty yards when, so help me, it started to sink. It just went down under us; it was one of those landing barges. There was another about twenty yards away and we swam to that. It was a tank-landing craft. A sailor started to pull me in, and someone hung onto my leg. The sailor pulled one way and the man in the water kept pulling the other. How the hell I got on board, I don't know. Then this boat started to sink. This was run by the navy, and boy what about that British Navy?"

"They're all right, Wally."

"The sailors went from man to man, grabbing helmets, guns, anything that was heavy and throwing all this stuff overboard to lighten the boat. We were very low in the water and we aimed for a small flak ship. Some of us got on that, and it took us to this destroyer."

"You got a story."

"I got a story," he admitted, "if we ever get back to England. That was no eight-inch gun before, was it?"

I told him it wasn't. I went above to see what was going on in Roberts' control cabin. He had taken off his coat and he was sweating a little but he was calm, alert. Listening to his crisp orders, you felt that he knew the score on every beach. No military strategy, no trick, no defensive maneuver would be overlooked in an effort to get those men off the beaches. Captain Hughes-Hallett came into the room. No one would have thought that he'd been through anything more strenuous than a maneuver. He and Roberts talked. They were like co-captains of a team, each respecting the other's opinion, each master of his own field, each complementing the other. They discussed the advisability of withdrawing the

181

men to keep pace with the timetable. They decided to withdraw them.

"I'd really do it as quickly as possible," Hughes-Hallett suggested.

Evidently the German air attack had become more intense. We learned afterward that the Germans had been taken so completely unawares that they had been forced to bring bombers from as far away as Norway and, of course, from Belgium and Holland. They had been forced to draw upon their "pool" far back in France, a "pool" reserved only for emergencies. But they finally did bring plenty of aircraft.

The atmosphere in the cabin was tense as the aides snapped orders into the microphones. All troops were to withdraw. This had only been intended as a left jab not as a knockout punch. It is silly to leave yourself wide open just to deliver a left jab.

I went on deck. Their shelling was fairly accurate. Our flotilla was not anchored; every ship kept moving so as not to present an absolutely stationary target. Flak ships (small craft carrying only anti-aircraft guns) kept spouting lead into the skies. The Spitfires darted here, there, everywhere. Sometimes, in pursuit of an

182

enemy plane, they left openings, and Dorniers and Focke-Wulfs slashed through. Our destroyer suddenly turned sharply and the motors sang a new tune. We were laying a smoke screen. The white smoke billowed out behind us. For eight miles we tore away from Dieppe, laying the smoke, and then dashed back, retracing our steps. The thick smoke settled and hung above the water, but at best this was only a temporary expedient. Wisps of breeze came to tear jagged holes in the smoke, to reveal us again to the enemy. Air Commodore Cole and Boyle came out and stood beside me. When an enemy plane was sighted, there was great and joyous yelling among the men with the four-inch guns. Then the thunder of them massaged your ear drums. The Germans never stopped trying. Time after time they'd throw squadrons of bombers, escorted by fighters, at us. Our fleet was in a radius of perhaps four miles. It would be difficult to drop a bomb without hitting some kind of a ship. The Spits kept slashing into the German formations, and ack-ack from fifty ships kept pitting the sky. It was a lovely day and the water was as calm as a dish of jello.

A barge came alongside and discharged about

thirty men—nearly all wounded. Our decks were quite crowded now with wounded. They lay there, stretcher to stretcher, and others leaned against gunwales and ammunition boxes. Two of the men who had just come aboard were American Rangers. They looked very young.

"Who were you with?" I asked a tall, blonde youngster.

"Commando No. 4," he said. He told me his name was Sergeant Kenneth Kenyon and that he came from Minneapolis. "It was bad on shore, but, my God, how those Commandos can fight! We were after a six-inch battery, and there was an orchard just before you came to it. Know what those Commandos did? They'd kneel down or lie down and fire; then stand up, grab an apple off a tree, and start firing again."

His pal was Sergeant Matchel Swank, also of Minneapolis. He had a shrapnel wound in his arm, but he laughed at it.

"I knew nothing could happen to me," he said, grinning. "I had a swell mascot with me—a Bible. It's a small Bible." He dug into his water-soaked clothes and came out with a sodden little book. "My father carried it all through the last war," he said. "And he never got hurt. So when I went

184

away he gave it to me and, believe me, I'll aways carry it. Pop's in the Army now, too. Sure, he's at Camp Dix. He's a Sergeant Major.

"How was it on shore?" I asked.

He made a face. "I'll tell you one thing, though. In training we used to be made to do a lot of things that seemed silly to us. Well, we know better now. Every bit of Ranger training we had came in useful today. You got to fight like Indians in this war, I guess. Well, we were trained for it, and any time we weren't sure we just watched our officers—those Commando officers. They're fighting men."

I walked aft. I had to pick my way through the wounded, who lay everywhere. I saw where the bomb had hit. The debris had been cleared away, but some blood remained. Several stretchers lay together, and the faces of the men lying there were covered. I came on four American Rangers squatting together, looking very calm and satisfied. The ages of the four wouldn't have totaled eighty. I started asking them questions, and they kept giving me that "sir" at the end of every answer, and I said, "For the love of God, I'm not that old! Lay off that 'sir' nonsense."

They looked puzzled and then I saw their eyes

travel toward my colonel's insignia. I'd forgotten them again. I explained, and they relaxed, and we sat down and they told me about it. They were four of the forty who had been picked for the raid. They were Staff Sergeant Kenneth Stemphen of Russell, Minnesota; Corporal William Brady of Grand Forks, North Dakota; Sergeant Alex Szima of Dayton, Ohio, and Corporal Franklin M. Koons of Swea City, Iowa. They were dead tired but they were happy and satisfied. They too had been with Commando No. 4. They'd done their job; they'd been under fire—tough fire —and had come through. A year before they'd been carefree kids, wondering what was at the neighborhood movie tonight. Now? Now they were men. They'd killed their Germans and they'd seen men die.

"I'd like to get hold of that louse back home," husky Corporal Brady said, clenching his big hands, "who used to say that the British couldn't fight. I never saw anything like the way these guys fight."

"They're not human," Szima broke in. "Listen, we'd all have been dead geese a dozen times, if it hadn't been for them officers. We're sissies alongside them."

186

"How about that sergeant major we carried out?" Koons* said excitedly. "He had a hole in his belly you could stick your first through. We were carrying him, and every now and then he'd yell, "Drop me. Drop flat." And we would, and by golly just then a burst of machine-gun fire would go over our heads. If we'd been standing up, we'd all be dead. He could sense when it was coming. And him only a sergeant major."

"How about that Lovat? He's something, isn't he?" Szima said chuckling, and they all chuckled at some secret joke too intimate to be shared by any civilian—even a civilian with colonel's markings on his shoulders.

"You know, I almost fell for that propaganda at home myself," Stemphen spoke for the first time. "Who the hell started it anyway? Talk about the Russians—if they're half as good as these British, they're terrific."

They sat chatting in the sun, ignoring the fire of our guns and the planes that sometimes dove low at us, and ignoring the shells that still came from the left flank. They chatted as men do after they've fought a good fight and it's all

* Later Corporal Koons was decorated with the Military Medal by Mountbatten.

187

over. If this was typical of the American army, we had nothing to worry about. I left them and walked back amidships. Air Commodore Cole, looking tired, was there and so was Boyle and two other officers. We stood there breathing the air which looked so clear and which tasted so bitter from the cordite and gunpowder.

10

THE Dorniers kept trying to get through the Spits, and occasionally one did. We had a dozen near misses. Usually the Dorniers paid for these close ones dearly. The destroyers we had with us kept circling, laying down smoke as heavily laden barges left the various beaches and headed out to where they could find transports or destroyers. One load after another of wounded came to us, and now the decks were literally crowded with men who lay quietly on

stretchers. The Luftwaffe, as though furious at
having been until now cheated of any real prey,
doubled its attack. It was then that the *Berkeley*
was hit. The *Berkeley* was a destroyer. A large
bomb hit it amidships. We didn't see the bomb
land, nor did we hear it, although the *Berkeley*
was only four hundred yards from us. The noise
from our own guns and from bombs landing in
the water near by had swelled into such a cre-
scendo of sound that it all melted into one ear-
splitting symphony of noise, so that one long
note could not be distinguished. But Hughes-
Hallett on the bridge knew, and we turned and
went to the help of the stricken ship. Motor-torpedo boats and landing barges, which weren't
too crowded, had surrounded the *Berkeley*. She
was listing to port and she had an odd, untidy
look about her. It was puzzling until you realized
that she had been struck amidships and her back
was broken so that her bow and her aft deck
seemed to be higher than her middle. You don't
have to slide from ropes on a sinking destroyer.
The deck is very low anyhow, and now, perhaps,
half-filled with water, the *Berkeley's* decks were
on a level with the Channel. It is hard to stand
helplessly by and watch anything—even a ship—

190

die. I thought of Colonel Hillsinger and of the
Wing Commander and of the British Major. I
wondered if any of them had been hurt badly.
The bomb must have been a big one. Destroyers
are sturdy things—hard to kill. Yet obviously,
Berkeley had received her death blow. We went
almost alongside. We weaved in and out of all
sorts of small craft watching men being pulled
from the water.

The British Navy was doing a job now. I doubt
if any man stayed in the water for more than
three minutes. Many were killed when that bomb
hit, but the last of the wounded were taken off.
Then, as though by a prearranged signal, the
smaller craft all retired, leaving us close to the
now deserted destroyer. She lay soggily in the
water but didn't sink. She lay there like a gallant
horse with a broken leg, pleading with its eyes
to be put out of misery. Our guns spoke briefly.
Jets of flame sprang from the *Berkeley* and then
smoke mercifully hid her last few moments from
us. Then the smoke cleared and the water bub-
bled furiously and a large patch of oil spread
out and calmed the bubbling water, and now the
Berkeley had reached the end of the road. She
lay far below on the bottom of the sea—the

191

only large ship the Luftwaffe had sunk during the day.

Many of the survivors were hurried to our destroyer. One of them was a British army captain. He was quite unhurt and he stood at the rail, looking at the patch of oil and swearing softly to himself. I asked him if he had seen Hillsinger. He nodded.

"They got him off," he said shortly. "I was with him when it hit. I didn't get touched. He did, badly. He had a new pair of boots on, you know."

"No, I didn't know. I only met him yesterday morning for a minute."

"He was kidding about his new boots," the British captain said. "He was very proud of them. We were on deck when the bomb hit us. It knocked me down but the bomb actually hit him. The ship listed badly to port—we were on the port side. I was unhurt and I went to help Hillsinger. He was swearing. The deck was level with the water, and there, so help me, floating three feet away, was one of Hillsinger's new boots. He was mad as hell and somehow he bent over and pulled the other boot off and threw it after the one that was floating there."

192

"You mean the blast from the bomb blew one of his boots off?" I asked, puzzled.

"Yes, it blew one of his boots off," he said, drawing a deep breath. "That was the boot that was floating there. It blew the boot off, all right. The boot floated there, and Hillsinger's foot was there too, inside the boot. Hillsinger is in a bad way, but he's a very brave man."

"He lost his leg?"

"He lost his leg," the captain said, tonelessly.

Our destroyer drifted away, and I went down again into the wardroom. Joe Crowther was still making bad jokes and doing a good job. He was going from man to man passing out and lighting cigarettes. He had Players with him. One of the wounded Canadians asked him to dig in his pocket and find some Sweet Caporals, the almost universal smoke with the Canadian army. Joe dug out a water-sodden pack of Sweet Caps.

"Now, look, mate," he said, hurt, "wouldn't you rather have a dry Player than a wet Sweet Cap?"

"No, I wouldn't," the wounded man growled. Cigarettes in peacetime aren't very important. I suppose if they stopped making cigarettes tomorrow no one would be the worse off. After a month

193

probably we'd all forget that we ever smoked cigarettes. But when you're in a tough spot or after you've endured a prolonged mental and physical strain, as these men had, cigarettes assume an importance far out of proportion to their actual worth. I remembered now the American cigarettes Jock Lawrence had given me when I had left him about twenty-four hours before. They were in my knapsack. I gave the Canadian a pack of Chesterfields and gave Wally Reyburn a pack of Camels, and I imagine that if I meet Wally twenty years from now he'll remember the cigarettes I gave him. Actually, drinks are fairly unimportant, and anyone who has been in the kind of spot we were all in there at Dieppe will tell you that strong hot tea gives you something that neither whisky or brandy can give you. I discovered that in Moscow, in Libya and in London bombings, and I rediscovered it there in the wardroom of the *Calpe*. But there is no substitute for a cigarette. It may be mostly mental—when you smoke a cigarette you get an illusion of normalcy that helps you take the beating that you are taking. I can't rationalize it or explain it; I only know that things seem easier when you have cigarettes and matches. This isn't merely

194

my own reaction; it's the reaction of every cigarette smoker I know. Our army is smart enough to know this, and our soldiers in Britain and in Northern Ireland are all allowed to buy cigarettes (at cost price) from their own canteens. The cigarettes are rationed in proportion to the supply. Soldiers would much rather have cigarettes than drinks. Our army is not a drinking army. Give our kids a few packs of cigarettes, a few cans of beer, a movie twice a week, and you won't have to worry about their morale. Fortunately, our officers, from General Eisenhower down, know this —and that perhaps is why our army is the most contented army in the world.

It seems pretentious for any reporter to make such a sweeping statement, but at one time or another I've been with almost every army in the world (except the Japanese Army) and the fine mental state of our men is so outstanding that even a reporter can't help but notice it.

The doctor came in to give the newly arrived wounded a once-over lightly. He was a sorry-looking mess. Apparently his nice white uniforms had long since gone, and now he wore a white shirt, lacking a collar, and his ordinary blue service trousers. I never saw a man who looked less

195

like a doctor, or who worked more like a doctor. He had some help now. A doctor who had been on the beach with the Royals had swum out and had been picked up by a barge that had brought him to us. So now we had two doctors—and about five hundred wounded. Every few moments, someone would stumble falteringly down the iron ladder and join our now jammed wardroom. It was strange how alike they all looked. Fear, pain, fatigue seem to paint a universal expression on faces which ordinarily might not be at all alike. Their faces were not white—but grayish. Their eyes were staring and they all moved rather jerkily like robots. I've seen punch-drunk fighters hanging around Stillman's gymnasium in New York who looked and acted as these men did and perhaps for the same reason. A fighter gets punch-drunk when his brain has received too many shocks. These men today had received too many shocks.

Then a huge man came down the ladder and into the room. He was quite all right, and he was smiling secretly to himself. There was something very familiar about him. He looked at me and grinned, as though he too were trying to remem-

196

ber where we'd met, and then he stroked his nose.

"You see, they didn't touch it," he said, and then I remembered where I'd first seen him. It was in an operating room at Queen Mary's Hospital at Roehampton, and I'd seen the great Thomas Pomfret Kilner, one of Britain's leading plastic surgeons, give him a new face.

"What's your name now, Butch?" I asked him.

"Smith," he grinned. "Good name for a Pole? Yes? The doctor was right. He said in one month I am ready for action—so here I am. I am with No. 4 Commando."

"You did all right today."

His big body shook with inward laughter. "We did all right today," he mimicked. "Oh, yes, we did all right. I got even a little bit," he added quietly.

This is a fiction story, I thought. This isn't happening. The whole thing is too fantastic. Twenty minutes ago I didn't watch a British destroyer die only four hundred yards away. Hillsinger's foot still in his new boot didn't float by him and he didn't angrily throw his other boot after it. These things don't happen. This is a

197

bad movie. This is one of those thrillers I read. It's a serial. It's anything in the world—but it isn't real. It's all too pat. There are too many artificial situations cropping up and then being settled too dramatically. How was it that Aeschylus and Euripides used to get out of tough spots? Remember every time their heroes and heroines seemed about to be overwhelmed they had a solution. DEUS EX MACHINA, *they called it. Sure a cheap device, but it worked for them. A chariot used to come down from heaven and just take their heroes and heroines away. It was like that now. I'd met this Pole two or three times and had listened to him, and he had told me what he was going to do. I'd forgotten all about him. And here he was. He'd done what he said he was going to do. It was all too pat. If I wrote all the things that were happening today and put them in a fiction story, the story wouldn't be believable.*

"My English is much better, no?" he sat down at the table. "A drink? I would like a drink—oh, very much I would like a drink. The water was quite chilly."

"You're all dry, though," Joe Crowther said, running a hand over his uniform.

"Been lying on deck," the big Pole said calmly. "The sun was warm. A lovely day, hey? Oh, but it was good on shore. It was so good. You know," he grinned at me, "you said, 'Take it easy, sucker. Rest up here for a few months. Good food, good beer, pretty nurses. Take it easy, sucker,' you said. Remember?"

"Sure, Pole, I remember." I laughed, and then I grabbed the bottle of brandy from Joe and handed it to him. I've got a weakness for Poles. I love the crazy devils. The war to them is a simple affair; kill or be killed. I wondered how many Germans this Pole had killed today.

We were jammed pretty tightly into the room now. The Pole wasn't wounded—just tired. He sat down on the table and talked about the last time we had met. The guns were still firing, and bombs landed close enough to make your stomach muscles tighten the way they do when you're scared.

"Much better on shore," the Pole grinned. "You like my nose?"

"It's a beautiful thing, Butch," I assured him. "Who picked that name Smith out for you?"

"I did," he said proudly. "I got papers to prove it. Herbert Smith, British citizen."

"You're the toughest-looking guy named Herbert I ever saw," I told him, and he laughed with delight. I never met a Pole I didn't like. They're very wonderful people.

"Hey, what's the matter with this fellow here?" Smith pointed to a Canadian who was lying on the table swathed in blankets. He had come in an hour or so before, half conscious, but when we got his clothes off we couldn't find any wounds on him. The doctor said he was suffering badly from shock. He was intoning now in a steady mumble, and sometimes the words rose and fell clearly, "Hail Mary, full of grace, the Lord is with thee . . . Blessed are Thou amongst women . . ."

"He's praying, Butch. Pay no attention."

Smith stuck the brandy bottle to the Canadian's lips. "Come on, soldier. Have a drink, soldier . . ." But the Canadian—his eyes half open but unseeing—continued steadily, "Blessed art Thou amongst women . . ."

The Pole shrugged his shoulders. "Some men

200

feel better when they pray. Me—I feel better when I drink."

Parenthetically, I might point out very hastily that if there seems to be a lot of drinking going on here, I've created an erroneous impression. Nearly every man who came into the wardroom was chilled through, and the brandy that Joe Crowther was handing out was strictly medicinal. No man had more than two or at the most three drinks of brandy. The doctor had ordered hot tea for them, but that direct hit had smashed the stove in the pantry and had broken most of Crowther's crockery.

Smitty sat there grinning, talking about his operation. Actually I knew more about his operation than he did. I'd seen it; he hadn't. So I told him about it right from the beginning. I'd seen the results of some plastic surgery done by Mc-Indoe and Gillies and Kilner and it was pretty amazing. I had wanted to do a story on wartime plastic surgery and had persuaded Kilner to let me bring my photographer into his operating room. I spent a whole day watching Kilner operate and his genius was apparent even to a layman. Then I'd become interested in the hospital (and the Pole who was now named Smith) and had visited it several times. I would never forget the first time I saw Smith.

Kilner was a handsome man, rather short and well groomed. He didn't much like the idea of having a reporter and a photographer in his operating room, but I persuaded him that the story I'd write might bring in some donations for the hospital. That broke all his resistance. I brought Robert Capa, my mad Hungarian photographer, with me and Capa's knack of making himself inconspicuous even there in the operating room met with Kilner's approval. I've worked with a great many photographers, but Capa is by far the best. By the time they wheeled the Pole in, Kilner and I were on good terms.

They had given the Pole a spinal anesthetic, and he lay there with a grin on his misshapen face. It was a very silly-looking face because the nose had been flattened and had traveled, it seemed, half way up his right cheek. Yet, even asleep, there was a grin on the Pole's face that somehow made you forget the hideous distortion of his nose.

"This chap was hit by a German rifle butt in Poland," Kilner explained. "It smashed the nose completely and spread it all over his face, as

202

you see. Somehow he escaped and made his way to England. He has been with a Commando outfit, but the medical people sent him to me to see what I could do. This nose all clogged inside with broken bone and cartilage is no good at all for breathing. They want me to fix it so he can breathe properly. But the Pole himself had an additional request. He had a photograph of himself taken before his encounter with the rifle butt. He wanted a new nose that would look nothing like the old one. I asked him why. He said that sometime he hoped to be dropped into Poland by parachute and he didn't want anyone to recognize him. It would be better, he said, if no one recognized him. So I am going to give him a new nose which, of course, will give him a new face. I am going to cut a bit of bone from his thigh and that will be used as the bridge for his nose. The nose will take the shape of this bit of bone."

Kilner began to work. A capable surgeon working calmly is a lovely sight. He didn't spill an unnecessary drop of blood. Capa, looking odd in his white cap and gown, made all sorts of shots from odd angles. I, too, was all in white and feeling like a master surgeon.

Kilner's quick, deft hands moved smoothly. Occasionally he called, in an unhurried, casual way, for scalpel or osteotome or for needles. He took a piece of bone from the thigh of the young Pole and then he carefully sewed together the long but neat-looking wound.

"He'll be stiff for a couple of weeks," Kilner laughed, through his gauze mask. "But he can spare that bit of bone."

Kilner sat down at a small white table under a strong light and called for chisels. He chipped and pared the bone until he was satisfied that it would fit. Then he went back to the table. He reached for a scalpel and opened the nose. He took out bits of broken bone and cartilage that had been smashed by the rifle butt. It was a rather bloody affair, but under the gas and ether the Pole slept, and not a muscle of his face even twitched.

One of the assistant surgeons nudged me at that point in the operation and, chuckling, pointed to my photographer, Bob Capa. We were all, of course, wearing white gowns, caps and masks, and Capa's usually ruddy face was now a pale gray. The doctor and I helped him out and into an anteroom.

204

"I'm blacking out," Capa moaned, and sure enough he went right out. Capa took atrocity pictures in China; he went through the Spanish war without being bothered by the killing he saw, and, to get a picture, he'd climb out on the wing of any aircraft in flight, but this was to much for him. The doctor had got a large glass of brandy, and he handed it to me. I put it to Capa's lips and then reconsidered. Brandy is very scare in London, and it seemed silly to waste it on an unconscious man. So I drank it myself. When Capa came to I told him I'd given him a large drink of very good brandy.

"Must have been good," he said. "I never felt it go down!"

Back in the operating room, Kilner was finishing up. He put the last small hemstitch in the wound, washed it carefully, and then asked me if I noticed any difference. It didn't look like the same man. No one would have recognized in this rather sharp-featured Pole the battered wreck who had been wheeled into the operating room an hour before.

"He'll be back in the army in a month," Kilner chuckled. "Made me promise I wouldn't do anything that would keep him out of action over a month. Pretty good men, these Poles."

Today plastic surgery is the science of rebuilding bodies, and its scope is immensely wide. During the day I watched Kilner operate; he didn't perform the same operation twice. Some involved dangerous operations, others, were, in his words, "routine surgery." There was a young dispatch rider who had been hit in the cheek by a bomb fragment. The scar had drawn up one side of his mouth so that he wore a perpetual, hideous leer. Kilner's knife worked busily for fifteen minutes, his needles for another ten, and the man would be normal.

I walked through the wards of Queen Mary's Hospital with Kilner, looking at post-operative cases. All were the result of either bombing or shrapnel or burns. Every type of skin graft was here, every type of war wound. In one woman's ward, there were eight women in bed.

"They all look cheerful enough," I suggested to the nurse.

"Yes," she said thoughtfully, "considering the fact that there are only five legs among those eight women—all blitz victims."

206

"It's Helen's eighteenth birthday," the nurse said to Kilner. "Would you care to see her?"

"Yes," Kilner said. "How is she?"

"Had a couple of bad days. Now and then she gets discouraged. Then, too, sometimes she remembers that night."

"Helen is our pet here," Kilner said. "She's eighteen today."

We found Helen enjoying the sun. She sat in a wheel chair and she wore a blue negligee of which she was shyly proud—a birthday present. I wondered if there was anything seriously wrong with her.

"Let's see how we're coming along," Kilner said gaily, and gently removed the loose new blue negligee from her left shoulder.

It was difficult not to cry out. Her left arm ended at the wrist, and, grafted to the lower arm, stretching to her abdomen, was a heavy tube of skin.

"Helen didn't need that skin on her tummy," Kilner said, laughing into the child's eyes. "So we attached it to her wrist, and now it's healed nicely, and soon we're going to attach it to her leg because she needs some nice new skin there."

207

He replaced the negligee around her shoulder and asked, "How is your other arm?"

"All right," Helen said, looking down at her right hand with interest, and then I saw that it was artificial. "I can work the thumb nicely. I can hold a fork or a cup easily."

"Soon we'll have another hand for you, and you'll be able to do anything you want," Kilner said.

"A bomb," he explained shortly, after we left Helen. "She lived in a town on the west coast. Lost both arms and her leg was burned badly. I have to do that graft to save the leg."

What Kilner was going to use to rebuild the pathetically broken body of the girl was what the surgeons called a Tubed Pedicle Flap. Once the wrist stump had healed, he cut a long strip of skin from her abdomen, sewed it in the form of a tube and attached it to her forearm. That had grafted perfectly. It formed a living, ten-inch bridge between her abdomen and her arm. This took only a couple of weeks.

Soon he would cut the skin flap off at the abdomen, and then graft that end of it to the damaged knee, because the burns she had suffered on the leg had killed the skin, and the blood vessels below the surface of the foot itself were receiving no life-giving blood. In time, infection would certainly set in. In short, the foot and lower leg would die and amputation would be the only remedy.

Once the skin flap had been grafted successfully to the knee (a matter of a few weeks), then the flap could be cut from the lower arm and spread over the lower leg. Once successfully grafted, life would return to the dying leg. To the layman, this seems a long-drawn-out process. It is, but barring unexpected complications, such a series of operations is usually successful.

Thousands of pilots whose faces and hands were burned to ugly, dead scar tissue have been returned to almost normal by the skill at skin grafting shown by the plastic surgeons of Britain. There was a time when plastic surgery was the bedraggled Cinderella of medical science. The public thought of a plastic surgeon as a sort of quack who spent his time lifting wrinkles from the parchment skin of aging dowagers or removing incriminating scars from the faces of public enemies.

Actually a plastic surgeon of the type of Kilner, Gillies or McIndoe is nothing but a highly qualified general surgeon who has applied his talents and experience to reconstructive and reparative work on every part of the body.

The science of reconstruction has advanced incredibly since the last war. It has advanced to such an extent that today Queen Mary's Hospital, in addition to victims of this war, has more than fifty casualties from the last. A jaw adequately rebuilt in 1920 will, because of the outmoded technique used at that time, now have lost many of its teeth. Routine bone grafting can be done to a jaw which has failed to unite properly. Hairless skin, probably from the upper arm, can be grafted on the lining of the cheek, and the contour built out where necessary with a wax mold.

I went to a hospital in Kent that was filled with blitz victims, most of whom were on the point of returning to the civilian life from which bombs had blasted them. I visited that hospital a year ago, just after the horrible May 10, 1941, raid on London. Every bed in it was filled, and patients lay in rows, in corridors, waiting their turn for the operating room.

Reluctantly I visited the hospital again, after a year, and found that a great many of the same women and children were there, but their eyes

210

had lost the vacant look they had had then, and now no sudden flashes of instinctive terror crossed their faces when remembrance came. A year had, to a great extent, banished the memory of terror, and if memory came, it came deep in the night when one was alone.

Legs and arms that were amputated in the last war as a matter of course, are now saved more often than not, but there are still thousands of amputations performed—for the alternative is death. Here at Queen Mary's, those who lost arms or legs had been refitted with artificial appendages, and there was not the slightest sign of despair on the face of a single patient. Plastic surgery or reparative surgery is closely aligned to orthopedic surgery. Once the stumps are healthy and alive with growing skin taken from some other part of the body, the task of fitting artificial limbs comes. The surgeons and the engineers have accomplished amazing things in the construction of arms and legs.

"Look at that," the doctor in charge chuckled, pointing to a ten-year-old girl. The youngster was skipping rope and enjoying it. "She lost her leg in a blitz only four months ago," he went on. "And we've fixed her up pretty well. You'd have

211

to look twice to know which limb is artificial. She can bicycle and she can walk, and now we're teaching her to skip rope. Youngsters are pliable and they adjust themselves easily.

"We have a gardener here I want you to see," he went on. "He was a patient of ours for a few months and wanted to stay on. We'll find him."

We found him grumbling because the weeds had strangled a few of his roses. The doctor asked him if he'd run down the garden path and then run back. The doctor added that he'd bet a shilling I couldn't tell which of his legs had been amputated. The gardener grinned knowingly (evidently this was a garden trick played on all visitors), cheerfully ran down the path, turned and ran back. He ran easily, evenly, and I couldn't tell which leg was artificial.

"The right one," I said. I was just betting on the law of averages.

"You're wrong, mate!" the gardener laughed, and he lifted his trousers legs a foot. Both legs were artificial.

"Of course, it takes time," the surgeon explained. "First, we have them exercise the right muscles to develop them. We fit them with artificial limbs to measure. Then they practice be-

212

fore a mirror. Adjustments can be made to the legs. Incidentally, they weigh only five and a half pounds each. As soon as they get the idea that they can actually walk, they want perfection. Our ultimate aim is to make them entirely unconscious of their artificial limbs. We discourage the use of canes, which reminds them of the loss they have suffered."

Artificial arms give even more scope to the surgeon and the engineer. This development has been rapid and most of it has come during the past two years. If you have one sound arm and hand, the artificial one is made to its measurement. The hand is made exactly the size of your good hand and, of course, is painted flesh color. The thumb is worked by a strong cord passed around the upper back of the patient. The thumb opens and shuts as he pushes his shoulder backward or forward. Such a hand can be used for carrying a suitcase, holding a newspaper or for any ordinary daily pursuits. For factory workers, there are all sorts of special gadgets attached by merely unscrewing the hand and screwing in the tool required.

None of this may be pretty to read about, but then, the war that has been waged against the civilians of Britain and Russia is not a very pretty war at all. Once you get accustomed to it, you don't mind the sight of wounded soldiers and pilots, but even the men on Kilner's staff confess that they never get accustomed or hardened to the sight of girls like Helen or of the eight women lying in the semi-private ward.

The war comes closer and closer to us in America each day, and if one is apt to complain about the rationing of tires, of gasoline and of sugar, the thought of the thousands of civilians still in hospitals in Britain trying, with the help of these magnificent surgeons, to rebuild shattered bodies which were never made to withstand the steel and iron of bombs, might come as a sobering thought.

The thought might banish the irritation we feel because we can't drive to the beach on Sunday. To date, the war has brought no suffering in America to any eighteen-year-old youngster like Helen or thousands like her.

I've gone on at length about Kilner and his work and the others in the hope that maybe someone with a few extra dollars will send it to Queen Mary's Hospital, Roehampton, London. If they had two thousand dollars they could build a small

214

motion-picture theatre and give the patients much needed mental relief.

I went back a few days after watching the Pole being worked on and met him. He was still grinning, huge and swarthy against the white of the sheets. Kilner introduced him to me. He had one of those unpronounceable, unspellable Polish names, which I never did get. I called him "Butch" from the beginning.

When we left the hospital he came to see me in London. Kilner's skill was evident by the fact that you couldn't notice a scar. His new, very straight nose was a thing of beauty and Butch was very proud of it. He was very happy about being with the Commandos. He would be useful. He spoke good German and French he said, and, in a pinch, could get by with Russian. He talked naively about what a fighting man he was; talked disarmingly, charmingly with no conceit at all. He just wanted to kill Germans.

And now here he was after five hours ashore. He had killed his Germans and he sat there relaxed and happy, talking about Lovat and Mountbatten and his British pals among the Commandos. He was a very happy man and when a Pole

215

is happy, he wants everyone with him to be happy.

"*Hail Mary, full of grace, the Lord is with Thee, Blessed art Thou among women and blessed is the fruit of Thy womb, Jesus.*" *He lay there quietly, with not a mark on him, and—yet something today had marked him and hurt him inside where it couldn't be seen. His lips kept repeating the loveliest of all prayers; a prayer especially dear to French Canadians. As long as the words came out his face was peaceful. Sometimes he'd stop and then you could see the reflection of some gigantic fight that was taking place inside—perhaps a fight between life and death or between hope and despair. Then the words would come "Holy Mary, Mother of God, pray for us sinners, now and at the hour of our death, Amen . . . Hail Mary, full of grace." For the first time the fingers, which had been clutching at the top of his blanket moved. They moved in a curious way. As he finished the prayer, his right hand moved to find his left hand and then the right hand withdrew a few inches*

216

> *to the side. It was puzzling and then, of course, I realized what he was doing. The Canadian was saying the rosary and fingering imaginary beads.*

"This fellow, he gets me nervous," the Pole said.

Young Boyle came into the wardroom. "The show is over," he said quietly, "Everyone is on the way home. Everyone but us. We're the only one left. General Roberts is going in toward the beaches to pick up any men who may be in the water."

"How long will we be here?"

"Half hour or so. At least until General Roberts is satisfied that there is nothing more he can do. We'll be here alone and we're sure to catch hell," Boyle added cheerfully.

This time Boyle's prophecy was good. We did catch hell.

11

FROM the deck we could see the ships re-
treating. Our destroyer turned in toward
the shore. Three ugly columns of smoke arose
from Dieppe. The men who had penetrated the
city had left their mark there. But we knew that
there were some men still on the beaches or in
the water close to the beaches. We went in as
close as the destroyer could go without grounding.
We were so close that they turned their machine
guns on us. We could hear the staccato bark of

218

the guns and then hear the bullets splattering on our steel hull. It was easy to find cover. We stood behind gun, screens or bulkheads and the bullets rat-tat-tatted against them. Machine-gun bullets could do not harm to a destroyer. Steel plates arose about neck high on the bridge and the men there crouched a bit to escape the bullets. Now and then someone spotted men clinging to wreckage or to rafts. We steamed slowly to them and they were hoisted aboard.

The shelling was bad now because they had us alone. Before there had been more than two hundred targets. Now there was but one—ourselves. The shells struck close and then threw up spurts of water. This all seemed so familiar now that we hardly noted it. We steamed past Dieppe and went to the beaches on the right. The Luftwaffe still kept trying. It seemed, in fact, as though they had redoubled their efforts, now that they had us alone. I was standing just outside the passageway amidships. Our guns were firing furiously, but suddenly above them came a new noise—a noise that having heard once you never forget. I looked up and to the rear. A plane had gotten through the umbrella of Spits. It was hurling itself downward at us, and four angry, baffled

219

Spitfires chased it. This was a Focke-Wulf 190. I stood, frozen, and so did the men around me. Boyle was there and Air Commodore Cole. The sound of a diving airplane coming at you is terrifying. It came from 5,000 to 300 feet in a few seconds; it leveled off and raked us from stern to bow with its eight guns and then it dropped a bomb. This was the first time a Focke-Wulf had ever been used as a dive bomber. The air was full of roaring noise, and I lunged backwards and through the passageway. I lay there on my back, listening to the world coming to an end. The concussion rang in my ears and the machine guns and cannon roared and then the sharp clang of bullets hitting and ricocheting from one steel object to another added to the sound.

I didn't know whether I'd been hit or not. I was dazed, lying there. Then I bit on something and spit out a gold inlay. I picked it up and put it in my pocket. Evidently the concussion had loosened it. The Focke-Wulf had roared away now, and our guns barked angrily and futilely after it. Hoarse voices were yelling. I got up shakily and walked the two steps to the desk. Two men who had been standing on either side

220

of me lay there on the deck. They were dead. A sailor helped Air Commodore Cole in. His face was covered with blood. Young Boyle stumbled past me, his hands to his neck. I went down to the wardroom with him. He had been hit in the neck and he had a head wound and they both bled a lot. We poured disinfectant on the two wounds and yelled for the doctor. He came and put temporary bandages on Boyle's neck and head. The blood seeped through them. He lay back in a big chair, half-conscious, his face drained of all color.

"This is a swell birthday present," he mumbled when I tried to give him a drink of brandy. Some thirteen hours before he'd mentioned that this would be his birthday. I'd forgotten. He was twenty-one now. He was a man. He waved the drink away.

"You're old enough to drink now," I kidded. He looked awfully shaky, and I was afraid he was going to cave in.

"Water," he said. There was a cup on the table. I rinsed it with water and then threw the water on the floor and filled the cup again. I put it to his lips. He spit it out and looked reproachfully at me.

221

"There was brandy in that," he said.

"So help me there wasn't. I rinsed the cup. I'll rinse it again." I did, and filled it with water and this time he swallowed it, though he could still taste brandy. The cup had been used for brandy before. Someone came in and said that Cole had gotten it badly. I fingered the little gold inlay in my pocket and for a moment was puzzled. I'd been standing with four men; two of them were dead, the two others seriously wounded. I had only lost a gold inlay. I tried to reach and hold some serious thought on this. What had I been saved for? But the thought eluded me. When you have close calls like that your reaction doesn't come until later.

You don't dramatize yourself or your reactions at the time; you do that later on, when you've had a chance to think about it and imagine re-actions you had then which you now think you remember. But I just stood there, puzzled, not thinking anything much, or feeling anything. I wondered idly whether I had flung myself through the passageway or whether the blast had knocked me through the door. It didn't matter—details aren't important in a spot like that. The only thing that matters is that you aren't hit.

222

After awhile I went on deck again. We'd been here nearly nine hours now and everyone was tired. There was no spontaneous shouting among the gun crews when they sighted a German plane. They merely loaded the guns and fired automatically. A body can take a terrible beating; a body is practically indestructible. But nerves can stand only so much. When nerves get frayed and the strain on them over a period of time becomes too much, the reaction varies. Some men become sullen and irritable; some become slightly hysterical. This has nothing to do with a man's inherent courage or stamina. The reaction is entirely involuntary. Our crew now moved about quite instinctively—everyone's nerves were worn. The wounded lying on the decks all had hopeless, resigned looks on their faces. They merely lay there, staring dully, talking to no one. An hour before they had been grim or relieved or perhaps smiling gently at thoughts of what they'd done ashore. Now there was nothing but dull apathy. Everyone knew that we were alone there in the harbor. Everyone admired Roberts for staying until he could get the last possible man off the beach or out of the water. Everyone admired his dogged courage, but this was an im-

223

personal admiration. Subconsciously now everyone was saying to himself, "For God's sake, let's
get out of here before we get it. They can't keep
on missing us forever." Not that they had actually missed us. We had received two direct hits,
and we still were afloat, which was something
of a miracle. We'd been thoroughly strafed by
that Focke-Wulf and its cannon and its machine
guns, and yet most of the crew were still alive.
But now we all felt that we were too vulnerable.
They didn't have to scatter their punches now;
they had only one target.

Our guns swung to port and idly now, because
this had happened a hundred times before today,
I watched the path of the shells and the bursts
which studded the sky like slowly opening black
blossoms. This plane was high over Dieppe, and
it seemed to be aiming for us. It was hard even
to be frightened now—you only felt a weary
apathy. Without curiosity, I again wondered why
our Spitfires didn't go after it. They kept circling
above us, ignoring the plane. The bursts from
our guns framed it. The plane had almost square,
stubby wing tips—a Messerschmitt-109. It came
closer, and now it was at a thousand feet gliding
down—not diving, hell bent, which was puzzling.

224

It wobbled too, and I wondered if fragments of our shells had hit it. But I didn't really care. It came directly at us, and it seemed a miracle that none of our shells hit it. We'd seen what happened when shell met plane before when the big Dornier came apart.

"It's one of ours," someone in the gun crew shouted, and above the Oerlikons and the pom poms stopped their barking. It was one of ours. It was a P-51 made in America; the plane which the British call the Mustang. It is almost identical with the M.E. 109. It is a nice aircraft, made by North American, powered by the Allison engine, and it carries four twenty-millimeter guns in addition to cannon. The airplane glided down to land less than fifty yards from us in the water. It was traveling slowly (for an airplane), yet it more than half submerged as it hit. The pilot shot from the cockpit as though he had been ejected from a cannon. He was aboard two minutes later, wet and spluttering a bit. He was all right, except for his right eye. That was closed, and blood ran from it. I went down to the wardroom with him. He was a young Canadian, a sergeant pilot, and he was very angry. He pulled off his wet clothes, and took the drink of brandy which Joe offered him.

"Very fine ack-ack stuff," he said sarcastically. "You fellows on these ships must have got a few Spitfires today, and you damn near got me. Can't those gunners tell one aircraft from another?"

"They had orders to shoot anything that came under 2,000 feet," I defended our gunners. "Didn't you all get that when you were briefed? The Huns might have a few Spitfires, you know, which they could use and drop right down on us. That was the form today—2,000 feet."

"Yeah, they told us to stay over 2,000 feet or risk getting pipped," he said. "But what the hell could I do? I got hit over Dieppe. A direct hit on my motor and it conked out. I either had to bail out over the city or try to sit down near you. So I tried that, and, my God, those ack-ack shells were close! What the hell were they using?"

"They threw the book at you: four inch, Oerlikons, and, when you got closer, pom-poms. By the way," I asked, to change the subject, "how do you like that aircraft?"

"A good aircraft," he growled defensively, as though to stop anyone from criticizing it. "Especially for our job, which is army co-operation. To-day we kept flying over the roads back of Dieppe,

226

spotting any reinforcement they tried to send up from the rear. When we saw anything we'd machine gun it and report. Down low this is the fastest airplane in the world. Up to sixteen thousand, I'll fight anything, yes, even a Focke-Wulf. I've flown them all, but I like this aircraft."

A great deal of nonsense has been talked and written about American airplanes. Most of this has come from the typewriter strategists who get their information from blueprints and specifications. As far as I remember, I've never seen the fighting pilots quoted on what they think of our airplanes. I've talked to pilots all over the world about the planes they fly (and their lives depend upon how well the planes are made and how fast they are and how maneuverable), and they look at the performance of airplanes in a different light than do the pilots of the typewriter keys. Once, I foolishly asked a wing commander, whose job was to test all American airplanes that arrived in Britain, "How good are American planes?"

He smiled and said, "When you go to some big, formal state dinner, you'll find perhaps half a dozen forks to the left of your plate. Each of those forks is there for a purpose. Each has a different purpose. There's the small fork for oysters. There's a large one for the roast; there's a middle-sized one for the salad. Now it's like that with aircraft. Each one is designed for a specific use. You can't generalize in regard to combat planes. You can only take each aircraft separately and ask yourself 'Is this doing the job for which it was designed?' On the whole, American aircraft do the job for which they are designed and, as far as the actual construction of them is concerned, they are the best in the world."

I knew that. I'd seen Lockheed Hudsons and Flying Fortresses coming home with wings and tails drooping and with hundreds of bullet holes in them. To date we have no fighter plane (unless it be the Republic P-47, not as yet tested in combat) to compare with the Spitfire-9 or the Focke-Wulf-190 for high-altitude combat. But these two great fighters are the culmination of years and years of designing, improving, of testing in actual combat. We haven't had those years to develop and test fighter planes.

But American planes are good. Consider our DB-7; the Boston and the Havoc, the British call them—the Boston for day fighting and light bombing, and the Havoc with modifications which fit it for night fighting. Pilots have told me that they

228

prefer it to any night fighter or light bomber,
prefer it even to the magnificent long-range British Beaufighter. As to the performances of the
aircraft, I know nothing. I do know what pilots
in Libya, Moscow, Malta and Britain have told
me. I avoid technical experts always. I'll take the
word of the man who flies one. In Britain, no one
liked our P-40's (Tomahawk). Most of the fighting over Britain, over the Channel, and over
France is at high altitudes. The P-40 couldn't
reach to the playground of the Focke-Wulf or the
Messerschmitt. But in the desert, where the fighting was nearly always at a low altitude, the boys
swore by the P-40's. For more than a year in
Libya, Air Marshall "Maori" Cuningham had
nothing but P-40's. He was very happy with them.
He called them his "Tommies," and, but for them,
Rommel long since would have established perhaps a permanent domination over that part of
Africa. Of course, the fighting was seldom over
10,000 feet in Libya. The Germans were trying to
bomb convoys of supplies and "leaguers" of tanks
and to hit such comparatively small targets they
had to come in fairly low. Their escorting fighting
planes had to come in low too, and the P-40's
did beautifully against them. On the basis of

what they did in Britain, one might say they were useless. On what they did in Libya (and in the Far East) they are magnificent. They are being used like the oyster fork—for the purpose for which they were designed.

You could go through the list of American aircraft and find that each one does the job it has been created to do. Consider our Boeing 17-E (Flying Fortress). When General Tooey Spaatz came to London to take command of our air force he held a press conference. He told us that his men would be in action within a few weeks. "Would they bomb Berlin?" we asked.

"No, not yet," Spaatz said, "Too long a trip in daylight, and I believe in daylight bombing."

The thousand-plane raids had just been launched by Air Chief Marshal Sir William Harris, and his bombers and we in London were all highly optimistic about the results. Spaatz did not minimize the value of night bombing, but he insisted that real, specific damage could only be done by what he called "pinprick" bombing, and that could only be done by daylight.

Since September 15, 1940, when 185 German planes were shot down over Britain in daylight, we had all thought that bombing by day was

230

obsolete. It just couldn't be done, we thought. The casualties would far outweigh the damage done. Yet here was General Spaatz talking blithely of sending American bombers over Germany and France daily. The casualties?

"We must expect casualties," Spaatz said, tight-lipped, "but, after all, in our job we have to take some risks."

For a long time Spaatz and Harris differed widely on the policy of daylight bombing. Harris didn't like it. Spaatz tried hard to sell him the idea. Finally, Harris told Spaatz to go ahead— he'd give him all the fighter protection he wanted. Spaatz wanted a lot of fighter protection. Harris probably winced when he heard how much, but he was game. The Flying Fortresses began their daylight raids. They went over daily for three weeks before they lost a single aircraft. They lost two that day—only because a fog had come up over the Channel and they missed the rendezvous with their fighter escort, and so had to go in alone. The Fortresses need plenty of fighter escort (three or four squadrons at least to one squadron of Fortresses), because they are very vulnerable for about two minutes. They use the magnificent Norden bomb sight, the greatest yet devised. But

231

a bomb sight only operates perfectly if your aircraft can be given a smooth, straight run into the target. If a Fortress can have a four-mile run, it is a ten to one bet to actually hit the target it is after. During that four-mile run it cannot dodge around or maneuver away from attacking fighter aircraft. The escorting fighters have to take care of it during that run. It would be easy to criticize the Flying Fortress (if you only read specifications, blueprints and figures) by saying that it only carried a third the bomb load of a British Lancaster or Halifax or Stirling. But then the Flying Fortress was designed for a different job than that done by the heavy, vulnerable big bombers. The Fortress is a flying porcupine; it has twelve guns and it can fight its way out of trouble. Let me repeat, I am only quoting pilots who fly these aircraft in battle. They love them; they swear by them; they think the Fortress is the greatest airplane ever made. They have terrific confidence in the airplane and they'll go anywhere, escorted or not with it.

Yes, you could consider each American aircraft separately (God forbid I try that) and find that it was doing a specific job. There is no such thing today as an all-purpose fighter or bomber.

232

Perhaps the Focke-Wulf or the Spitfire comes closest. Neither, for instance, is a dive bomber, but in emergencies each can be equipped with small bombs and be used as such, without fear that the wings might drop off. Of course, they wouldn't dive as steeply as a plane designed for vertical mayhem (like the Navy Curtiss Hell-diver), but they would be extremely useful. Anyhow, the daylight bombing by our air force so impressed Harris that a month after our first big raid he tried it himself—with Lancasters. No doubt, daylight bombing will play a bigger role from here on than it has previously, and it might be remembered that the idea was born in the minds of Generals Arnold, Spaatz and other of our air leaders.

To return to our wardroom. Now there were about forty men in the room, and they took up every bit of space. They lay on the table; they lay on the floor and on the settee which ran the width of the room; they sat in chairs; and they stood leaning against the steel walls. No one talked much. The strain was beginning to tell, but no one cracked up. Boyle lay back in his chair, and the blood still seeped from his neck and his head. I asked him how he felt.

"I was supposed to take care of you," he grinned weakly. "A fine conducting officer I turned out to be."

"You'd feel better with a drink."

He shuddered. "No." He was just allergic to alcohol, I guess.

Our four-inch guns kept roaring and occasionally our pom-poms began to bark. Each gun had a sound of its own. The four-inch had a throaty roar, the Oerlikon had a rather high-pitched snarl that was very disconcerting, but the pom-poms bothered us the most. We knew they were fired only when the enemy planes were fairly close— their range didn't equal that of the other guns. Pom-poms are usually arranged in clusters of four guns, and when they fire it sounds like a hard fist banging a table at regular one-second intervals. It would take all of us a long time to get that monotonous, and somehow ominous, pounding out of our minds.

"Let's go home, for God's sake, let's go home." A wounded Canadian lieutenant stood up suddenly. "I've had enough," he sobbed. "Let's go home."

"Have a drink, man," Joe Crowther soothed.

234

"We've all had enough, but the Skipper knows what he's doing."

The Canadian drank deeply from the bottle. The rest of the men looked away from him, as though not to notice his outburst. He had broken the rules. Something inside of every man in that wardroom was crying out, "Let's go home! For God's sake, let's go home," but no one would allow that cry to be uttered. No one of the forty men in that wardroom felt brave. Yet each one endured it, despite a strong conviction that we would get it sooner or later. Each one endured it, and each one had a corner of his heart that was brave, and the cumulative bravery of all lent itself to each. Had anyone of us been alone there, below the water line, we would by now be jibbering idiots. We would have had nothing to draw on, no reserve from someone else. It's always like that when you're in danger. It's hard to face it alone without cracking up. But if others are with you, you draw on their strength, as they draw on yours.

The Canadian had buried his head on the table now, and he was muttering a bit wildly. He talked as though he were drunk, but he wasn't drunk. An hour before the doctor had stuck a needle into his arm to kill the pain from his wounded leg. It wasn't a very bad wound, but shrapnel had torn his knee cap, and there isn't much flesh around a knee cap to absorb pain or shock. Morphia seems to react differently on different people. It puts some to sleep. It lulls others into forgetfulness. Apparently it made this officer a bit delirious.

"It was awful on the beach," he sobbed, speaking to himself. "They got our tanks. They got us all. The bullets came from everywhere. It was awful, do you hear?"

He stood up again, looking around the room, wild-eyed. No one said a word. What could anyone say? Wally Reyburn stood up and slapped him on the back. "Sure, it was awful. It was awful for everybody. Take it easy, chum."

The officer sat down again. The guns which had been quiet for a few moments all began to go at once. We all became tense and, then, above the guns, came the explosion of a bomb, the ship keeled far to port and trembled; a rush of water from the pantry swirled into the room and we held our breaths, and once more the noise rang in our ears. The ship veered sharply to starboard.

"It was a miss," Crowther's voice rang out.

"Never touched us, mates. Just shook us, and that water is from our sprinkler system. Watch out, or your cigarettes will go out."

This time he was telling the truth. It was a near miss. A very near miss, and now we were zig-zagging rather madly.

Matchel Swank, the young American Ranger, came into the wardroom, looking down at his arm in a puzzled way. He had rolled his sleeve up and his forearm was covered with blood. It didn't hurt, he said; in fact, he didn't remember getting it. Joe Crowther gave him some first-aid and I got the reliable bottle of brandy.

"A drink will do you good," I told him.

He looked at the bottle curiously. "What is it?"

"It's brandy—good brandy—and it'll warm you. It will make your hair curly, is good for the teeth, lengthens the years of your life, will fix flat feet, is fine for the complexion and makes child-bearing easy."

He looked suspiciously at the bottle, took a drink, choked, spluttered, spit it out and asked plaintively, "Haven't you got any Coca-Cola?"

Forty men—nearly all wounded—were jammed there in the wardroom, and they were all quiet. If a novelist could have taken down the thoughts which ran through the minds of each he would have the book of the century. Of what was each thinking? Certainly not of the future. Reading the future is for palmists, for sky gazers, for charlatans. Anyone can read the future and these men knew that only two alternatives lay before them —life or death. You could toss a coin with a fifty-fifty chance of being right. Each, no doubt, was thinking of the past.

Some looked vaguely puzzled. What were they doing here? How had they gotten into this mess? Few of these men were professional soldiers. A year before they'd been working on farms, in mills, at school—they were leading normal lives in which murder was something out of a Sunday supplement. Murder and violence—these happened not to you but to someone else. Now violence was part of their lives and it was unnatural. If only one had the gift to read their minds. Their faces were for the most part blank, but who knew what stories their minds were telling them? Some no doubt were drawing strength from these stories out of the book of their memories. Were they thinking of their families or of one particular girl until then half-forgotten? For the moment their weariness and pain had banished the fine,

238

healthy emotion of hatred which had sustained them on shore but which by now had exhausted itself. There is no room for hatred when you're tired and bleeding and frightened.

The Chief Engineer stuck his head in the doorway. "We're headed for home," he said briefly, and you could almost hear the relief exude from the forty men in the room. I climbed up to the deck to see if it were true. It was true. The three columns of smoke still arose from Dieppe. We turned slowly and faced the open Channel. Our flotilla was out of sight. We were alone, except for the Spitfires. Our engines quickened their beat. It was a beautiful late afternoon. The water was still calm and sun-drenched. The word had spread, and the walking wounded were laughing now, and the faces of the men who lay everywhere changed from apathy to interest. We had a long trip ahead of us and we knew that the Luftwaffe would not give up easily, but we were headed for home.

From the lower deck come the incongruous screech of a bagpipe. A huge Canadian was walking back and forth, jerkily playing the weird, screeching instrument. He was a member of the Essex Scottish and he had brought his pipes

239

ashore. A bullet had gone clean through his bags, but now he had patched up the holes, and was really going to town. It's the first time I ever enjoyed bagpipe music. It belongs in the open on a destroyer, whose guns are banging, because you don't get the full impact of it then. The music was our farewell to Dieppe and the French shore. The white cliffs got smaller and smaller, the beaches receded, and, finally, only three thin spirals of smoke were left to mark Dieppe. Dorniers and Focke-Wulfs kept trying. We had two more near misses and twice Dorniers went down in flames not far from us. We caught up with our flotilla. It was a brave sight. All sorts of ships lumbered along. Barges, self-propelled, still laden with men; fast motor-torpedo boats; barges being towed by transports; flak ships, looking pert and impudent with their guns pointing skyward. We caught up and passed them all. This was fine, we thought. We'd head right for home and our fast destroyer could make it in a couple of hours. But that wasn't the idea. Oh, no. Once again we had to be first through that mine field. The mine field looked very innocent now in daylight. It was hard to believe that a careless slip to either right or left would mean that we'd be

240

blown sky high. But this was no time to be making careless slips. And Hughes-Hallett was not the kind of man to make careless slips. On we went and then we were through it.

The Channel is wide at this point. For a long time we were out of sight of land. Hours passed and now the sun, having seen enough this day, balanced itself on the horizon. Far ahead we saw a thin line and then there was England. The coast thickened and there were cliffs emerging from the water, and we knew that we were not far from Newhaven. We were in mine fields now, but they were British mine fields and our navigators knew the lanes. We never traveled in a straight line for very long. We zigzagged through the lanes, and our Spitfires, flying lower now that darkness was approaching, kept near us. There were twelve of them with us still, flying in widely separated flights of four each. They circled us, flying at 500 feet, and occasionally a flight would cut directly over us, and the Spits would dip their wings in salutation. We were going home, but there was no jubilation, no happiness on board. Everyone was too tired, and men were thinking of comrades who'd been left behind. We didn't know yet how many had been left behind.

General Roberts walked out on deck. He looked tired now. He leaned over the rail, looking down into the water.

"It was tougher than you figured, wasn't it?" I asked.

He drew in a deep breath. "Yes," he said slowly. "It was tougher than we figured. They had more stuff there than we knew. Our casualities were heavy."

One lone Dornier appeared from nowhere. We all looked at it, amazed. It was flying fairly low. Our guns began roaring again, and the Dornier caught sight of the Spits. The Dornier did a right-about-face and three Spits went after it. The Dornier had a start of about three miles. The Spits closed in, and I found myself, incredulously, rooting for the Dornier, a feeling I was ashamed of. But he was so outnumbered, so outgunned. Whether he got away or not, I don't know. The Dornier and the Spitfires disappeared in the dusk, and we continued on.

Then we split up. We and one other destroyer kept on straight, and the rest of the fleet headed for Newhaven. The Spitfires split up too. Four of them stayed with us and the rest went with the other ships. The darkness was closing in now, quickly, as it does at sea, and it was welcome. Our destroyer lunged on, groaning and complaining, but never faltering. We were headed for Portsmouth, and that would be another three hours. But it was a quiet three hours, and that blessed quiet was very welcome.

12

IT WAS dark when we reached Portsmouth. By now wounds had begun to hurt: the merciful, deadening anesthetic of the shock had worn off. The wounded had lain still for so long that they had forgotten that pain was lurking just beneath the surface of their wounds. The movement of walking, the jolting of the stretcher as men stumbled in the dark brought the pain out into the open. Wounds held lightly together by the bandage pads and court plaster reopened,

244

and mutters of angry pain spread. These men swore softly at the pain, swore at the unaccountable weakness of these bodies which, having withstood and smothered agony all day, now had relaxed their fight and had allowed pain to take the upper hand. Men were hungry and thirsty and conscious that they hadn't been out of their clothes for two days. Miraculously, our destroyer found her berth; miraculously, because the night seemed an opaque wall of black. There is no better blacked-out place in Britain than Portsmouth. We stumbled tiredly off the ship. A tall, silent figure stood at the end of the gangplank. General McNaughton, Commander in Chief of the Canadian Army, had come to meet his men. A buzz of excited comment ran from stretcher to stretcher, and weary men lifted their heads to catch a glimpse of the popular McNaughton.

The organization was magnificent. No orders were necessary. Men slipped aboard silently, picked up stretchers bearing wounded and walked down the gangplank. Nurses stood on the pier and, as the wounded walked off, each nurse grabbed an arm and led the tired men to waiting ambulances. There was no confusion. Wally Reyburn and I walked off together.

"Ambulances are right here, ready to go," nurses and doctors told the men who stumbled off the destroyer. "You'll be at the hospital soon—plenty of beds and clean sheets—hot tea all ready . . . Nothing to worry about now . . . " Huge ambulances moved, phantomlike, up to the gangway, were loaded, and then moved away. Officers flashed tiny flashlights and the pinpricks of their shafts now and then showed faces contorted in agony. Two large ambulances were reserved for the dead, and then they brought up two more. We had about fifty dead with us and about seven hundred wounded.

Reyburn and I bumped into a familiar figure, Larry Audrain, the official photographer of the Canadian Forces. He had come to meet the troops, but he couldn't photograph them here; no flashlights were allowed on the open docks at Portsmouth. He led us to a hut where headquarters had been established.

"You're a natty figure of a man," he said to Reyburn. Reyburn was clad becomingly in socks, shoes and one heavy blanket. He was carrying his still wet uniform under his arm.

"What about Drew Middleton or Larry Meier or John McVane of NBC?" I asked Audrain.

246

"Haven't heard about any of them," Audrain said. "They were all scheduled to go ashore."

"McVane's wife had a baby about a month ago; they shouldn't have allowed him on the show."

"You can't keep guys like John off a show like this," Audrain said.

"I'm worried about Drew," I told him. "He once played football at Syracuse, and he thinks this war is a football game. Any time he's on an operational trip he is apt to run ahead to catch a forward pass."

"They have rooms reserved for you at the Queens," Audrain said. "I have a car. I'll send you along in that. And a car is to pick you up at eight in the morning to drive you to London. They don't want you guys to go by train—you might talk too much."

We were too tired to resent even that. Reyburn and I climbed into a staff car. We started off into the blackness of the Portsmouth streets. The driver turned to us and said, "You know how to get to the hotel? I'm new down here."

Neither of us knew. We drove slowly along until we heard footsteps. Then we'd stop and ask directions. There was no moon tonight and the streets were heavy with darkness.

"Portsmouth had three alerts today," our driver told us cheerfully. "We shot down four of theirs but they dropped some bombs. Killed quite a few, too."

"That's fine," I told him. "I suppose you expect another raid tonight."

"Oh, yes," he said quite cheerfully. "After Dieppe they'll want some quick revenge and they will certainly figure that some of the raiding force came here to Pompey. I dare say we'll catch it tonight."

"That's all we need," Reyburn said. "We've had a hell of a day and now we think we're safe and we'll probably get bombed all over again."

I remembered the song "Over The Hill to the Poorhouse" and the line of comedian Jack White, who used to say, "The poorhouse? As though it weren't tough enough, they had to put a hill in front of it."

We found the Queens. It was a solid square of opaque black, silhouetted against the slightly less dark of the night. No light showed, and we wondered if we could rouse anybody. We rang the bell and the night man appeared. He ushered

248

us in, took one look at Wally in his blanket and then gave a startled look at me. For the first time I realized that my uniform was spotted in a dozen places with blood—none of it mine.

"This fellow is a Canadian Indian," I told the night man. "They always dress like that."

"Is there any chance of getting some food?" Reyburn asked. It was 2 A.M. now.

"Why, bless you," the portly night man smiled. "I know what a day you've had. Heard all about it on the wireless. Now you go upstairs, have a nice hot bath and I'll see what I can do."

He gave us the papers which all day had prominently played up the raid; had in fact given practically a play by play report of it. We had our baths and they felt awfully good. We climbed into two huge beds and read the papers. We were amazed and gratified to see that the RAF had downed at least 150 German aircraft. The papers, we thought, were a bit optimistic as to what the raid had accomplished, but then they hadn't heard about our casualties as yet. By now we knew that they were heavy. The night man came with a large plate of ham and cheese sandwiches and a pot of steaming tea. As Reyburn reached for the teapot, he winced, and the night man noticed that he was in pain. I told him about Wally's wounds and made Wally turn over so I could show off the wound that he'd never be able to see himself. The night man hurried away and brought back clean bandages and iodine. Feeling every inch the master surgeon, I poured the iodine on the two wounds and then Wally, yelling because the iodine hurt, said, "Not so much. You're wasting that iodine."

"What the hell, it isn't your iodine," I told him cheerfully. "It's all free, have some more."

We lay there almost too tired to sleep and I think unconsciously waiting for the alert. But the alert never came and suddenly I came out of a dream in which I was back in New York at Toots Shor's restaurant arguing amiably about the Dodgers and the Cards, to find a large, motherly woman shaking me.

"It's seven thirty," she said sternly. "Here's your tea, and I managed to get a bit of tomato and bacon for you."

Grilled tomato and bacon had replaced bacon and eggs as the standard breakfast in Britain. Eggs are very scarce. Wally and I weren't much refreshed by our sleep. We'd only had about four hours and we were both groggy. His wounds were

250

irritating. They weren't serious if they didn't get infected, but bits of shrapnel lying beneath the surface of your skin are apt to be unpleasant. We dressed in our filthy uniforms and then the alert came. You never get accustomed to the sound of the siren. I've heard sirens in London, Plymouth, Coventry, Liverpool, Manchester and a dozen other cities in Britain. I've heard the sirens in Moscow and in Cairo and never got used to them. Now in New York we have a practice siren every Saturday at noon and even that one scares the hell out of me. When Wally and I heard that siren in Portsmouth, we wanted to get out—but fast. It would be awfully silly to survive a show like Dieppe and then get hit by an ordinary bomb.

We drove to London in two hours. The country was peaceful, lush-looking, and it seemed hard to believe that only a few hours before we'd been at Dieppe. Both of us were quiet on the ride, mentally writing the stories we'd typewrite after we'd left Mountbatten's headquarters. The best way to write a story is to do it before you sit down at a typewriter. By the time we arrived in London, both of us had our stories done. The actual typewriting wouldn't take long. The press conference was on the fourth floor of Mountbatten's Combined Operations headquarters. It was a long walk up, especially for Wally, whose wounds were smarting now. We walked into the big conference room. Drew Middleton, freshly shaved, in clean civilian clothes, was there, grinning.

"We were worried about you, sucker," I told him.

"I had a hell of a time," Drew laughed. "I was on a motor launch and we toured all over. Couldn't get ashore though."

Larry Meier of INS was there, still in his dirty uniform, with a bandage on his face. He had been wounded in the face and chest but again it was shrapnel and not serious. John McVane was there quite unharmed. So was Gault MacGowan of the *New York Sun,* Ross Munroe of the Canadian Press, A. B. Austin of the *Daily Herald,* who had covered the show for all the English newspapers, and Robert Bowman of the Canadian Broadcasting Corporation. It developed that only Reyburn, Munroe and Austin had been able to land.

Mountbatten walked into the room, accompanied by General Robert McClure of General Eisenhower's staff. We couldn't get a hint from

Mountbatten's face as to how he felt in regard to the raid.

"General McClure has something to say to you men first," he began, and Bob McClure got to his feet. He was one of the most popular of the American leaders. McClure was always co-operative whenever we wanted anything in the way of facilities.

"General Eisenhower has a request to make of you men," McClure said. "We have just received reports from America as to how the newspapers are treating the Dieppe operation. It is not, of course, the fault of you men; none of you have sent stories as yet. Nor is it the fault of the other correspondents here because we have checked the stories they sent. However, many American papers came out today with headlines which would indicate that Americans had a big part in the show. One paper had a headline which merely said, "Americans land in France." You men know just how many Americans we had on the raid— only a token force. We had forty American Rangers and a few observers. General Eisenhower is thoroughly embarrassed by the way our boys have been played up, when actually their part was infinitesimal. General Eisenhower asks you to send a service message to your offices explaining that this was a Canadian and British operation. There were only a few Americans and a few free French on the raid."

I think each one of us felt a sense of shame that newspapers at home, just to sell a few thousand extra papers, would—by writing misleading headlines—completely distort the news of the raid. McClure emphasized the fact that only a handful of papers had done this, and he repeated that not one story sent by any correspondent in London would have led anyone to believe that anything more than a token force of Americans had been on the raid.

"We haven't been able yet to check up on how many men, if any, we have lost," McClure went on. "So we'd rather you didn't mention the exact number of men we had on the raid. It would be giving the enemy information. But General Eisenhower would appreciate it if you would tell your offices that only a small detachment of our men accompanied the Canadians and British at Dieppe."

Mountbatten then briefly told us what we could and could not say about the operation from a military security standpoint. We could not mention the number of troops engaged; the number of ships which took the men across; we could not mention the attitude of the French civilians the men met on shore. Then one of Mountbatten's assistants took over.

"We broadcast to France yesterday morning," he said, "telling the French people that this was merely a raid—not an invasion. We asked them not to co-operate or aid our troops in any way, knowing that when our men left, the Germans would punish them for any help they gave us. You have all been talking to troops who were ashore. You know that the attitude of the French was very friendly. The raid was a great boost to their morale. But we'd rather you mentioned nothing of that. It would give the Huns a chance to execute many of them.

"As to the raid itself, we haven't all the particulars yet. The navy did a splendid job of getting our troops over there on schedule time. The meeting with that German tanker entering the harbor was unfortunate, and the heavy losses sustained by the Canadians who landed on the left flank were caused by that accident. It is true that we did not accomplish all of our objectives. It is also true that we did accomplish our main

255

purpose. We sent a fairly large naval force to Dieppe, kept them there for more than nine hours and suffered the loss of only one destroyer. We lost some tanks, but we hardly expected to get all of our tanks off after the operation was over. When it came to a choice of saving tanks and jeopardizing the lives of men, we decided to destroy and leave the tanks and avert any additional loss of life. The raid worried the Germans considerably. This morning their radio has given two different versions of it. One version was that it was a hurriedly prepared raid made necessary by the presence of the Prime Minister in Moscow. In fact, the German radio says that the raid was virtually ordered to show Stalin that we were trying to do something. The second version given by the German radio is that the raid was intended to establish a permanent bridgehead; that it was, in fact, the opening of the so-called second front. As you men know neither of these versions is correct.

"The RAF lost ninety-eight planes, which is unfortunate, but the casualties are not heavy when you consider what the RAF accomplished. Thirty of these pilots were saved. Actually our fighter planes broke the power of the Luftwaffe in this theatre of the war. The Luftwaffe had to draw upon its pool and had to bring aircraft from as far away as Norway. We haven't the final figures yet, but we know that the fighters officially downed at least 91 German aircraft and, in addition, there are two hundred others listed as "probables." The raid taught us a great deal, all of which will be of value in subsequent operations. Are there any questions?"

There were. We asked a hundred questions and Mountbatten answered them all without reserve, some on the record, most off the record. Then we hurried back to write our stories. I went to the Savoy. Ed Beattie of the United Press was waiting and so was my furious secretary, Betty Marais.

"You were going on an inspection trip with General Eisenhower!" she said scornfully. "I told everyone, too. Imagine, lying to me like that."

Beattie had a cable from his New York office. The United Press, because of the vagaries of the drawing, had no man on the raid, while both the AP and INS did have men. The UP wanted me to write a story of the raid for them. *Collier's* had agreed. I got to work on that and in the midst of it, Arthur Christianson, the editor of the *Daily Express*, phoned. He too wanted a story—but immediately. I wrote both of them, and then sat down to do my real story—the story for *Collier's*. I did it in two installments and it was ten o'clock at night before I'd finished. It had to go to Jock Lawrence for technical corrections. I phoned him and he came to the Savoy and read it there. It was a relief to have it done and off to the Press Wireless. I knew it would be in New York within an hour or so. And then I was tired. I'd been at the typewriter for eight hours. I went to bed and left a call for the following Tuesday. But I couldn't sleep, of course. Finally I took two sleeping pills and had nightmares for fifteen hours.

Trips across the English Channel these days are apt to give you nightmares.

13

THIS chapter was, I am sure, read by the Office of Combined Operations. Whether or not they agree or disagree is their prerogative. However, there is nothing in it that would endanger home security, nor is there anything here that I learned "off the record" or by virtue of the somewhat privileged position I had on the raid. It is always dangerous for a layman to assume the role of "military expert," and, quite properly, informed military and naval authorities of Britain

259

and America frown on such assumption of pseudo-authority. We reporters do ourselves, and nothing is more laughable to us than the writings of civilian "military experts" far from the scene of the operation.

Although Mountbatten's office has passed this chapter, there is in that no implication that the Office of Combined Operations approves of my views on the raid or that Combined Operations vouches for the truth of what I write. Some of what follows is necessarily in the field of conjecture. I am going in for a spot of Monday morning quarterbacking. It is the kind of thing Mountbatten and all real military leaders dislike. They are quite right, too.

However, the Dieppe operation was much more than an isolated raid and the significance of it can, to some extent, be understood even by a layman. What did it accomplish? Why was it not completely successful? Why was it important? How did it affect the North African campaign and how will it effect subsequent military operations? I realize that any selectee who has spent two months at Camp Dix knows more about military tactics than does any war correspondent in the world. However, the lessons learned at Dieppe were so obvious that even a layman who was there could learn them. The reasons that the operation was not conclusive are obvious, too, and these reasons may be commented on, I trust, without transgressing the necessary and quite reasonable rules of military censorship.

The raid was originally conceived by Mountbatten and his staff. At first it was to be an all British show, and Mountbatten and his staff had a plan which varied a bit from the plan of operation finally adopted. In every raid the Commandos ever perpetrated the element of surprise and the method of striking where the Germans were weakest were the two prime factors. Not that Combined Operations picked soft spots (St. Nazaire was one of the best-defended places on the French coast), but the Commando theory is to rush in on the flanks instead of launching frontal attacks which, in view of the fact that the attacking force is always outnumbered in such operations, would be suicidal.

It had been intended in the beginning to make it, for the most part, a British operation, using Commandos and British troops who had been given special training. General McNaughton, however, was insistent that his troops be given a chance to get into action. This was understandable enough. For two years Canadian troops had been billeted in Britain, doing nothing more exciting than occasional maneuvers. They were thoroughly fed up. They were well trained, in great physical condition, and they wanted to fight. Boredom is a greater enemy of troops than disease, discomfort or German guns. Activity is the only antidote for boredom, and McNaughton pressed his claim that Canadians bear the bulk of the action in the next big operation. The British War Office reluctantly agreed; reluctantly, because if the show went badly it would give American critics of Britain yet one more chance to chortle, "See, the British allow others to do their fighting for them."

This had happened before. In Libya, whenever there was a South African or Australian victory, the prowess of the Dominion troops received great acclaim in America. When a British regiment did something worth while it was ignored. This was chiefly the fault of the British War Office which would rather preserve the anonymity of its regiments and take for granted their heroism. The British War Office is not exactly streamlined—mentally. No one in America ever realized that

262

75 per cent of the troops engaged in the Libyan campaigns were British and that about that same percentage of the total casualties were British— not South African or Australian or New Zealand. Anyhow, the War Office agreed that the next big operation be a Canadian show.

Mountbatten in effect said to Generals McNaughton and Roberts, "Here is my staff. Use it as you will. Use its experience and its knowledge of Channel conditions." Mountbatten's original plan was considerably changed, and a frontal attack decided on.

When General Roberts saw that his frontal attack was faltering he brought reserves from his flanks and poured them into the withering fire that those attacking Dieppe itself had to face. Mountbatten's way (judging by past performances and his military philosophy) would have been to strengthen his flanks and in effect make them the main focal points of attack. Most of the losses were incurred in the frontal attack.

This was due chiefly to the fact that the information received from intelligence was ten days old. During that time additional guns were installed and the position of others changed. The RAF photos showed the two six-inch gun batteries at Berneval and at Varengeville. They did not show the heavy guns in Dieppe itself or reveal the fact that the Germans could (and did) manage a very heavy cross fire that was bound to destroy men or tanks who entered the city. The RAF photos did not show all the mortars back of the shoreline, all set to lob shells right onto the beach. Their range had long since been fixed. Nor did the RAF photos show that the tobacco factory in Dieppe and the Casino were virtually armed fortresses. And, of course, even the best photographs do not disclose hidden machine-gun nests or camouflaged blockhouses bristling with guns.

The opposition met was much greater than had been anticipated. In all, about 10,000 men were engaged in the operation. This, of course, included the fairly large naval personnel and the RAF pilots. More than a third that number were lost, killed or wounded. On the face of it, this might indicate that the raid was a complete failure— but nothing could be further from the truth. It was not the success we all hoped for on the trip across the Channel, but, taking the long view, the Dieppe attack can only be classed as a definite and useful operation which accomplished almost

264

everything that the military leaders hoped it would accomplish.

As Mountbatten said, it proved that a naval force could spend considerable time in a well-defended, enemy-occupied port without the loss of anything except expendables; tanks; landing craft; invasion barges; flak ships; men. It may be cruel to say so, but military leaders must think of men as expendables. Not well-trained pilots, or navigators or specialists, but the ordinary soldier or sailor is an expendable. It is true that he can only be expended at a certain rate.

The raid completely broke the back of the German air force in France. The raid helped the Russians in several ways. To begin with, the Germans had to believe that Dieppe was merely one raid in a series—that others would follow. The fact that the raid was launched against perhaps the best-fortified spot on the coast, meant that no other spot was immune from attack. All of these places had to be and were immediately reinforced. The Germans in France, following the Runstedt plan, have their main defensive force some forty miles back of the coast. Good roads lead to the coast, and their theory had been to have plenty of mobile units ready to be rushed coastward

265

from this forty-mile position. Because of the great RAF work in covering the roads leading to Dieppe, the Germans have had to revise their plans. Today they have moved more troops to the coast itself. No doubt they had hoped to relieve their hard-pressed forces in Russia by sending several divisions from France to their aid. The Dieppe raid made them give up this plan.

I mentioned that the back of the Luftwaffe was broken that day in August. Supporting evidence comes from the fact that except for the Canterbury raid when twelve Germans were downed, not one real aerial attack has been launched on Britain since Dieppe. The magnificent Focke-Wulfs destroyed that day certainly were not expendables, nor were the German pilots who were killed. Two weeks after the raid, I spent a few days with one of our Eagle Squadrons. They were then going over France on daylight sweeps, hitherto dangerous and difficult operations. But now they were jubilant. They were being allowed to pulverize shipping, troop trains and ack-ack batteries with only negligible opposition from the Focke-Wulfs. Germany could not afford to lose any more of them.

Dieppe taught the British, Canadian and Amer-

266

ican chiefs of staff many lessons. Many of them, it is true, were of a negative nature, but were useful all the same. Suppose, as the Canadians attacked, a few thousand parachute troops had been landed behind Dieppe and behind the flanks at Berneval and Varengeville. There is no doubt that they would have put any blockhouses, any hidden machine-gun nests, any airdromes, and most of the mortars out of commission. While they were engaging the Germans behind the city and behind the flanks, Commandos and the Canadians would have had a much easier time landing. It may have been coincidence, but two and a half months later, General Eisenhower brought plenty of parachute troops with him to North Africa and used them to grab airfields and rear positions.

Suppose 300 British and American bombers had gone to work on Dieppe and on the flanks just before daylight on August 19th. Two hours of intensive bombing would certainly have had the effect of considerably weakening the German positions and of further endangering the morale of the German troops. Many, many of them would have been in shelters and not behind guns when the actual landing of our troops took place. Air Marshall Sir William Harris—the story is—did not think that a preliminary bombing would have been effective. The gun emplacements were small targets to hit at night. The German defenses were not so concentrated that bombs could find them and wipe them out. However, I am sure that a real bombing would have almost eliminated immediate resistance. It may be a coincidence, but General Eisenhower had his air force do plenty of preliminary bombing before his troops did any frontal attacking in North Africa.

Suppose we had used dive bombers at Dieppe. There are two schools of thought on the question of dive bombing. The British Air Ministry does not believe in the efficiency of the dive bomber except at sea. Dive bombers, the RAF says, are of use only against positions which are not well defended by ack-ack guns and fighter aircraft. And, they add, that any position worth attacking is well defended by ack-ack guns and fighter aircraft. If you point to Crete, they merely say that Crete was an undefendable island; that it had no anti-aircraft guns to speak of and of course no fighter protection at all. This is the viewpoint of the Air Ministry and no layman has the right to dispute it. But the thought remains that dive bombers could have put those nasty six-inch gun

268

batteries at Berneval out of commission fairly easily. There would have been casualties among the dive bombers, of course, but the extermination of that battery would have been worth some casualties. However, the question of dive bombers in Britain is pretty much an academic one. Britain has virtually no dive bombers. She ordered some from America back in July, 1940, but never obtained delivery on them. Actually our navy was given priority on dive bombers and, as events developed, very sensible priority it was too. Our dive bombers have done marvelous work in the Pacific. However, in the establishment of any second front in France or Italy, a layman's observation would be that dive bombers would be a magnificent weapon. The dive bomber considered as the extension of the artillery, the range of which is so limited, is, I am sure, part of General Eisenhower's future plans.

Soon a second front will have to be established in France. Just as General Eisenhower studied every move, every part of the Dieppe operation, so will the men in charge of that second front use Dieppe as a textbook. General Eisenhower certainly benefited by Dieppe in planning the North African operation. In fact, he was big enough to

269

ask Mountbatten and his staff to help him plan
that venture. All of the knowledge of tidal waters
and currents and weather and coast topography
which Mountbatten's office had in regard to northern Africa was handed over to Eisenhower.
Mountbatten had already considered the idea of
a large-scale raid against the places finally
attacked by Eisenhower. He had made a plan
and turned that over to General Eisenhower.
How much of that plan General Eisenhower used
I do not know. Three days after the Americans
had landed in northern Africa, Eisenhower sent
Mountbatten a cable of thanks for his help. By
inference he was thinking of the men who had
died at Dieppe; they had helped. In answer-
ing Eisenhower's cable Lord Mountbatten said,
"Yours was the greatest combined operation of
all time." One of Eisenhower's most important
aides, Brigadier General (now Major General)
Lucien K. Truscott, was with us at Dieppe. Nothing that happened there escaped his keen eyes.
He later played an important part in the North
African venture, leading the force which stormed
Port Lyautely. It would be a safe guess to say that
many American lives were saved that day which
might otherwise have been lost had not General
Truscott learned the lessons which Dieppe taught.

The Story of Dieppe

When the second front comes in France, it is
hardly likely that the Dieppe pattern will be used.
No doubt a less rigid, more flexible plan will be
followed. To begin with, that big assault will
probably not be a single frontal attack. There is
no doubt that combined United Nations forces
will strike in several places at once. (This statement is not based on information received or on
"inside tips," but merely on observation and common sense.) Such an attack will split up the German air force. The whole Luftwaffe will not be
able to concentrate over one attacking point as
they did at Dieppe. During that day we probably
had 600 (a rough estimate) enemy aircraft attacking us at one time or another. When (and if)
our forces strike in perhaps ten spots the Luftwaffe will have to scatter into ten defending
forces. It is much easier to handle sixty enemy
aircraft over you than 600. If paratroops have
grabbed German airports behind the coast, the
efficiency of the Luftwaffe will be greatly
decreased. Even the great Focke-Wulfs have to
refuel quite often, and, if they have to fly far to
the rear to find unmolested airports, their range
and the time they can stay at the spot of operation
will be considerably lessened.

Dieppe proved that a second front in France

is now feasible where a few months ago it would have been suicidal. We didn't know whether or not we could get a really large naval force through German mine fields in the Channel; we didn't know whether or not we could land tanks on the French coast. Because of Dieppe we now know that we can do both of these things. You can't fight German troops without tanks. Nearly every failure in Libya and certainly the failure of the French army at Cambrai and Sedan was caused by inferiority in numbers and efficiency of French, British and American tanks.

Today the American tanks have proven themselves to be among the best in the world. Too, we are building and have in mass production the best tank destroyer ever conceived by military men. When our second front starts, not a handful of tanks and tank destroyers (such as we had at Dieppe) will be landed, but a thousand of them will be landed. They are absolutely essential in any big-scale attack.

When our second front begins we will have to feed a huge army of men; we will have to keep a stream of ammunition, medical supplies, gun replacements flowing into the bridgeheads we establish. This can't be done by ships alone. Huge

272

cargo-carrying planes already on their way to Europe will have to be used to ferry supplies from Britain to our bridgeheads. One of the new huge cargo planes making seven trips a day across the Channel can ferry as much as one small supply ship.

This second front is more urgently needed than ever. Today the Russians are doing magnificently in a military way, but men just back from Moscow and Kuibyshev say that the civilians of Russia (actually there are no civilians in our meaning of the word) are badly up against it.

All of the best food and clothing is of necessity sent to the front. Even factory workers in munition and aircraft plants are eating ersatz hamburgers and very thin cabbage soup. They are wearing threadbare clothes and millions have been unable to buy either shoes or coats this past year and a half. Russia cannot afford a long war—we, of course, can. We can try to wear Hitler down with a reasonable chance of doing that. But that won't help Russia, and Russia, having borne the burden of the war in the European theatre, needs help badly. Only a second front in France will force Germany to withdraw large forces of troops, tanks and aircraft from Russia. An attack on Italy and

273

Greece will not have this effect because long ago the Germans visualized the possibility of such a campaign and prepared for it. Right now (February, 1943) there are thirty divisions of Italian and German troops in Greece and at least that many in Italy. Many of these are crack Italian Alpine troops and at least twelve divisions are well-rested, well-equipped German troops. Originally, Hitler hoped to send these men to Africa. They are set up as African divisions, which means that each division has close to 20,000 men —a total of about a half million troops. An attack on them will not cause Germany to drain her forces in Russia. Only a second front in France will do that.

I remember listening to a captured German colonel in Libya about a year ago. He was a suave and superior colonel, who treated his British questioners with condescension. It was as though he were a teacher explaining problems to school children. He had every full confidence in the eventual outcome of the war. One of the British questioners asked him, "Colonel, what do you Germans think of your Italian allies?" Amusement glinted in the eyes of the colonel as he answered,

"Oh, we regard them much as the Russians regard you British and the Americans."

It was a cynical but perhaps truthful statement. A year ago I never heard such sentiments expressed in Russia. But the Russians are notoriously polite. And then they held high hopes that their allies would somehow make a move which would take some of the pressure from them. But during the past year neither Britain nor America has done much to relieve that pressure. It is quite true that until recently neither of us was in a position to really do anything. But now we have grown stronger; each day adds to our strength. The time has come to achieve the impossible, just as the Russians achieved the impossible at Stalingrad. The time has come for striking in France, in Norway, in Holland. None knows this better than does our General Staff. No more offensive-minded group of generals exist than our own military leaders. They know that today it's smart to be offensive. Eisenhower has proven that. They know that they must strike soon or risk the loss of the advantages which Russia's great fight has given them. Men like Mountbatten know this, too. And there is no doubt that the great offensive will not be long in starting. Not that I am trying to suggest this to our generals. General Eisenhower, so far as I know, never told a correspondent how to run his typewriter; it is only fair that we refrain from telling him how to run his war. War is one game in which the amateur has no right to interfere with the professional. We Monday morning quarterbacks would never think of telling a doctor how to operate, a lawyer how to plead a case or a pilot how to fly a plane—but the columns and editorial pages of our newspapers and magazines are filled with amateurs telling our professionals how to run the war. When I say that an invasion of France is the only way we can really help Russia (and thus help ourselves) and eventually force a decisive issue with the German Army, I am only repeating what a hundred American and British war leaders have told me.

When that occurs the name of Dieppe, now almost forgotten, will be remembered. Perhaps the critics who called the raid a failure will then realize that no great lesson learned is ever forgotten, that no great and gallant attempt such as the Dieppe operations could ever be called a failure.

Of course, not everything ran smoothly at

276

Dieppe. I am sure that scenery bogged down, that actors forgot their lines, that costumes failed to arrive even at the dress rehearsal of *Hamlet*. Dress rehearsals never run entirely smoothly, but they are very necessary to the success of the first night. And Dieppe was never intended to be anything but a dress rehearsal.

Two days after the raid, British and American "military experts" (out of uniform) were explaining the operation in profound and patronizing manner. They told just what Mountbatten had intended to do; they explained wherein he and the Canadian leaders went awry. The *London Daily Mirror* carried a few words on this subject which seem pertinent even now. They were in the form of a verse which read:

> The "armchair strategists," dear men,
> Are busy at their desks again.
> They see, as words flow from their pens,
> Their purses fatten.
> And all our plans when we invade
> By them are openly displayed.
> They know much more about this raid
> Than does Mountbatten.

Dress Rehearsal

They deal at lengths with many schemes
That have existence in their dreams
And use the paper up in reams.
But why read through it?
For time is costly, paper dear
The lesson of Dieppe is clear
And summed up very briefly here,
Is: We can do it.